Same Sex,
Different States

Same Sex, Different States

When Same-Sex Marriages Cross State Lines

ANDREW KOPPELMAN

Yale University Press   New Haven and London

Printed in the United States of America by Sheridan Books,
Ann Arbor, Michigan.

Library of Congress Cataloging-in-Publication Data
Koppelman, Andrew.
Same sex, different states : when same-sex marriages cross state
lines / Andrew Koppelman.
     p.   cm.
Includes bibliographical references and index.
ISBN-13: 978-0-300-11340-2 (cloth : alk. paper)
ISBN-10: 0-300-11340-4 (cloth : alk. paper)   1. Same-sex marriage
—Law and legislation—United States—States.   2. Interstate
agreements—United States.   I. Title.
KF539.K67 2006
346.7301'68—dc22   2006010460

A catalogue record for this book is available
from the British Library.

The paper in this book meets the guidelines for permanence and
durability of the Committee on Production Guidelines for
Book Longevity of the Council on Library Resources.

10 9 8 7 6 5 4 3 2 1

To Val, whose marriage has crossed too many state lines

Contents

Acknowledgments

In the course of writing this book, I have benefited from more conversations than I can possibly remember, so the following is a very incomplete list of acknowledgments. I begin with special thanks to the law librarians without whose assistance I could not have produced this manuscript: David Gunn of the University of Texas (presently of Hunton and Williams, Washington, D.C.) and Marcia Lehr of Northwestern University.

Thanks to Regina Schwartz for suggesting the title, to Mark Gergen for helping to devise the hypotheticals in Chapter 5, and to Peggy Pascoe for sharing her research on cases involving interracial marriage. William Eskridge Jr., Peggy Pascoe, Louise Weinberg, Russell Weintraub, and members of the Northwestern Faculty Workshop read parts of the book, and Lea Brilmayer, Erin O'Hara, Michael O'Malley, and Joseph Singer read the entire manuscript. All provided very helpful comments.

My children, Miles, Gina, and Emme, constantly brought home to me the high stakes of this debate.

Thanks to Valerie Quinn, my wife, who has followed me from Washington, D.C., to New Haven, Naugatuck, Princeton, Cambridge, Princeton again, Austin, Chicago, and Evanston.

This research was supported by the Northwestern University School of Law Summer Faculty Research Program and the Kathleen M. Haight Fund. Special thanks to Dean David Van Zandt for his unflagging support.

Portions of this book previously appeared in the following articles:

"Dumb and DOMA: Why the Defense of Marriage Act Is Unconstitutional," 83 Iowa L. Rev. 1 (1997)

"Same-Sex Marriage, Choice of Law, and Public Policy," 76 Texas L. Rev. 921 (1998)

"Interstate Recognition of Same-Sex Civil Unions after *Lawrence v. Texas*," 65 Ohio State L. J. 1265 (2004)

"Interstate Recognition of Same-Sex Marriages and Civil Unions: A Handbook for Judges," 153 U. Pa. L. Rev. 2143 (2005)

"Against Blanket Interstate Nonrecognition of Same-Sex Marriage," 17 Yale J. L. & Feminism 205 (2005)

Introduction

If there is one thing that the people are entitled to expect from their lawmakers, it is rules of law that will enable individuals to tell whether they are married and, if so, to whom.
—*Justice Robert Jackson*

Americans are profoundly divided about same-sex marriage. In the 2004 elections, voters in twelve states approved referenda banning such unions. But in Vermont and Massachusetts, two states in which same-sex unions are recognized, the pro-recognition factions increased their numbers in those states' legislatures.

Each side now is striving for total victory. Proponents of same-sex marriage want a judicial declaration, preferably by the U.S. Supreme Court, that recognition of same-sex marriage is constitutionally required. Opponents want a constitutional amendment banning any state from recognizing such marriages. Neither side is going to get its way soon; consensus on this emotional and divisive issue is a long way off. In the meantime, we need to find a way to live together.

The consequence of our moral divisions need not be hysteria or chaos. If each state could confine its own answer within its own borders, so that, for instance, same-sex marriage stays in Massachusetts and other states do nothing to harm same-sex couples in Massachusetts, then we could easily live with our differences. Even the strongest opponents of same-sex marriage can tolerate the fact that it exists somewhere, even somewhere nearby. When Canada recognized same-sex marriage, no one in the United States called for military intervention.

But people move around.

It's easy to say that Utah and Massachusetts can each have their own rules. But sometimes it's not clear which state's rules should apply. Can Utah residents get married on a weekend trip to Boston and then expect Utah to recognize the marriage? And what happens if someone from Massachusetts is hospitalized in Utah, and the hospital needs to know who is legally authorized to make the patient's medical decisions? We need to know where one state's laws end and another's begin.

The disagreements over interstate recognition are almost as profound as those over the underlying marriage issue. Some think that recognition of same-sex marriage is demanded by the provision of the U.S. Constitution that requires states to give "full faith and credit" to each other's legal judgments. If that were true, then every state would have to recognize the same-sex marriage of any of its residents who can manage a day trip to Boston. Others think that states should adopt a blanket rule of nonrecognition, under which same-sex marriages would be void outside the jurisdiction that recognized them. But if this were the case, people in same-sex marriages could desert their dependents with impunity and, by crossing a border, free themselves of all obligations of marital property and child support. They could even marry other people without telling those people about their still-existing marriages.

Both of these positions are wrong. Fortunately, well-established legal rules exist to help us navigate this thorny landscape. These rules are unfamiliar to many, but they are urgently relevant. This book explains what they are and how they can help us. They do not offer a path to universal harmony, but they can help show how people who are irreconcilably divided in their opinions can still live together. *Federalism,* a system in which different state laws can reflect different ideas of "the good life," is a classic American idea. It can serve us well here.

This book is about law and public policy. It is not a guide for same-sex couples who are trying to figure out what their legal rights are and how to protect themselves in the present legal climate. Other books provide that help.[1] Nor is it an attempt to resolve the moral disagreement over same-sex marriage. In this book, I take no position on the issue.[2]

Choice of law is a body of legal doctrines that explain what a court should do when a problem involves the laws of more than one jurisdiction. It offers a set of fairly clear and workable rules, specifying the bounds of each state's legitimate authority. And it offers a reasonable resolution of today's culture war over same-sex marriage.

No choice of law cases have ever arisen in American law concerning same-sex marriage because until recently no state had ever recognized such marriages. There have, however, been equally profound moral disagreements concerning marriage. They have involved differences in state laws regarding incest (for example, marriages of first cousins), marriageable age, remarriage after divorce, and above all, interracial marriage (what its opponents called "miscegenation"). In none of these situations were states compelled to recognize other states' marriages. (Even when the Supreme Court struck down every law against interracial marriage in 1967, it did not do so on this basis. It held instead that such laws were unconstitutional because they were racially discriminatory.) But in none of these cases did the courts adopt a blanket rule of nonrecognition, either.

The most revealing of these disagreements concerned interracial marriage. This issue involved an exceedingly strong public policy: the southern courts regarded marriages between blacks and whites as "connections and alliances so unnatural that God and nature seem to forbid them."[3] The statutes prohibiting such marriages were worded at least as strongly as those of the recent laws against same-sex marriage: they usually declared them "void" and "prohibited" and punished their celebration with criminal penalties. Yet even in this charged context, the courts rejected the blanket rule of nonrecognition. In nearly every case that did not involve someone trying to evade their home state's laws, the southern courts recognized interracial marriages. The overriding policy was that interracial marriages could not be celebrated by the forbidding state's own residents. If each state could determine the marital status of its own residents, then it was possible for states with very different moral views to live together, and for individuals to know what their rights were.

This book argues that a similar solution is the best way to find a truce in the war over same-sex marriage. Such marriages, when celebrated by people who make their home in Massachusetts, should be recognized everywhere those people happen to travel. But citizens of Utah should not be able to evade that state's marriage restrictions merely by spending a day in Massachusetts.

I am not predicting what courts will do in these cases. There is not much case law in this area yet, and courts face pressures from many directions. It is impossible to know how they will respond to these pressures. But there is a right legal answer, and this book argues that courts ought to follow it. Here I will look at law, in H. L. A. Hart's famous phrase, "from the internal point of view." Any set of rules, Hart writes, can be viewed from the "external" point of view of an observer who does not accept them and simply wants to understand how they affect other people's conduct. But judges are expected to consider rules from the point of view of "a member of the group which accepts and uses them as guides to conduct."[4] Following the law means, in part, deciding like cases alike, by following relevant precedent when new cases arise. The system of precedent, Hart observes, can generate "a body of rules of which a vast number, of both major and minor importance, are as determinate as any statutory rule."[5] The relevant precedents here are cases involving interracial marriage. Courts should follow them.

Whatever external political pressures courts may face, they will always, one hopes, feel some obligation to just do their jobs and follow the law. In the case of interstate recognition of same-sex marriage, if they follow the precedents that I describe here, then they would sometimes recognize these marriages. Again, this is not prediction: it is always possible for courts to disregard the law, and sometimes they will. All one can say in the face of such behavior is that courts should not act in a lawless fashion without powerful reasons, and that the opposition to same-sex marriage has not cited any reasons of that weight.

This book begins by introducing the general themes of the debate and becomes more detailed as the discussion unfolds. Chapter 1 provides an overview of the history of the same-sex marriage controversy, showing how we got to our present impasse. Chapter 2 examines the rules of marriage recognition and the nature and scope of exceptions to those rules. Chapter 3 describes legal precedents from the controversy over interracial marriage. Chapter 4 examines the interests of states that have strong public policies against recognizing same-sex marriages. Chapter 5 considers and rejects the simplest way of implementing a state public policy against recognition of same-sex marriages: a blanket rule of nonrecognition. Chapter 6 surveys a number of possible choice of law rules that occupy a middle ground between automatic recognition and blanket nonrecognition. Chapter 7 proposes a set of fair and workable rules to determine when, and when not, to recognize same-sex marriages. Chapter 8 examines the federal Defense of Marriage Act (DOMA) and shows why this statute has had almost no effect on the law. Chapter 9 examines the state statutes, enacted in forty states, that deny recognition to same-sex marriages. Chapter 10 considers what choice of law can and cannot do, offering a reasonable response to an intractable moral controversy.

Much of what I say relies on the miscegenation cases, which are, obviously, a morally problematic set of precedents. A word is in order about why they should have any weight at all.

Among the differences in state marriage laws, same-sex marriage is unique today in the degree of moral passion that it arouses. There have, however, been other times in American history when marriages of a certain kind produced comparable revulsion in some quarters. If we are to learn anything from earlier cases, we must place ourselves in the shoes of earlier judges. We have to give some weight to public policies that we either would repudiate (as with the ban on remarriage after divorce) or would endorse (as with the prohibition of marriage between cousins) with far less strength than was once assigned to them. The most useful such line of cases is that involving the most morally repellent of the public policies: the one against interracial marriage. Such marriages provide the best analogy to today's controversy because they provoked more vehement antipathy than any other kind of marriage that states disagreed about. Moreover, these cases form a fairly consistent pattern, from which a set of rules can be drawn. If we suspend, for the sake of the argument, our objections to the substantive laws in question, we may find a certain wisdom in these rules. The Jim Crow judges were terribly wrong about many things, but they did understand the problem of moral pluralism in a federal system, and we can learn something important from the solutions that they devised.

There is also value to this exercise precisely because these cases are so strange to us today. They compel readers to think about how to give weight to policies with which they have no sympathy. If you are reading this book, then you are probably already interested in the issue of same-sex marriage. You probably have an opinion about how this issue ought to be resolved. You may think that same-sex marriage is a moral imperative, or you may think that it is a moral abomination. On the other hand, I'm pretty sure I know what you think about laws against interracial marriage. People on both sides of the same-sex marriage issue agree that the miscegenation prohibition was immoral and unconstitutional. If you can put yourself in the situation of past courts that grappled with the issue, then you may find it somewhat less difficult to perform a similar exercise with respect to today's differing state interests regarding same-sex marriage.

A federalist solution, in which different states are free to pursue different policies, offers something important to everyone. For people who oppose same-sex marriage, it offers security against the wholesale importation of institutions they find morally repugnant. Same-sex marriage can be confined to Massachusetts, for instance, and need not migrate elsewhere. For gay people, it offers relief from being national scapegoats. It is not in the interest of gays to make opponents of same-sex marriage feel that they must act aggressively in order to protect their local conceptions of marriage. At the end of that road is an amendment to the U.S. Constitution banning same-sex marriage.

The federalist answer cannot be a permanent one, of course. Sooner or later, one side will prevail in the culture wars over homosexuality. But it will take a while. (We took three hundred years to reach consensus on interracial marriage.) In the meantime, people need to know what their rights are. And federalist reasoning, which presumes that radically differing moral views may each have their own legitimate field of operation, can remind us that people whom we think morally obtuse are nonetheless our fellow citizens. Mundane legal answers will not bring us to the promised land, but they may make our present abode more habitable.

I

How We Got Here

Robert Kaufmann met Walter Weiss in 1948. Within a year, they had moved in together. Robert was an heir of the Kay Jewelry fortune, but he had no interest in business. He wanted to be an artist. Walter encouraged these interests and eventually ran the household; oversaw the cooking, cleaning, and entertaining; answered the mail and telephone; paid the bills from Robert's bank account; and found doctors when Robert was ill. Robert turned out to be talented. By the time he died, eighty museums had accepted his paintings for permanent display.

Beginning in 1951, Robert made a series of wills, each of which increased Walter's share of his estate. The last of these, drafted by a prominent New York City law firm, left nearly everything to Walter. It was accompanied by a letter to Robert's family, which he signed in 1951. It declared that before meeting Walter, Robert was "terribly unhappy, highly emotional and filled to the brim with a grandly variegated group of fears, guilt and assorted complexes." Walter, it said, had encouraged

Robert to submit to psychoanalysis, which had benefited him enormously:

> Walter gave me the courage to start something which slowly but eventually permitted me to supply for myself everything my life had heretofore lacked: an outlet for my long-latent but strong creative ability in painting . . . , a balanced, healthy sex life which before had been spotty, furtive and destructive; an ability to reorientate myself to actual life and to face it calmly and realistically. All of this adds up to Peace of Mind. . . . I am eternally grateful to my dearest friend—best pal, Walter A. Weiss. What could be more wonderful than a fruitful, contented life and who more deserving of gratitude now, in the form of an inheritance, than the person who helped most in securing that life? I cannot believe my family could be anything else but glad and happy for my own comfortable self-determination and contentment and equally grateful to the friend who made it possible.
>   Love to you all,
>   Bob

In 1952, Robert executed a document granting Walter the types of powers that a legal spouse would have. Walter was given exclusive power over Robert's corporeal remains and the authority to make all funeral arrangements. If Robert was incapacitated, Walter was given the power to consent on Robert's behalf to the performance of any operation he deemed necessary. The instrument provided that Walter was to act as "though he were my nearest relative . . . and that his instructions and consents shall be controlling, regardless of who may object to them."

In April 1959, sleeping alone in his Florida home, Robert died in a fire.

Robert's family had never liked Walter, and they had resented his interference with their business decisions while Robert had been alive. Robert's brother, Joel, sued to have the will set aside on grounds of undue influence. A will can be set aside for undue influence, the court explained later, if the beneficiary "internalizes within the mind of the testator the desire to do that which is not his intent but the intent and end of another." The scenario that voids a will on this basis is one in which the testator has become a sort of marionette, whose own will is completely overborne by that of the manipulative beneficiary. A typical example is when a feeble ninety-eight-year-old man signs a will disinheriting his family and leaving all his assets to his nurse.

There were two jury trials, both finding undue influence, and the appellate division of the New York courts held that there was enough evidence "to find that the instrument of June 19, 1958, was the end result of an unnatural, insidious influence operating on a weak-willed, trusting, inexperienced Robert whose natural warm family attachment had been attenuated by false accusations against Joel, subtle flattery suggesting an independence he had not realized and which, in fact, Weiss had stultified, and planting in Robert's mind the conviction that Joel and other members of the family were resentful of and obstructing his drive for independence."

Robert's letter was held to be "cogent evidence of his complete domination by Weiss." The court of appeals affirmed, finding evidence that Robert "was pliable and easily taken advantage of" and "that there was a long and detailed history of dominance and subservience between them." Robert's carefully drafted will was ignored.[1]

The Shifting Cultural Landscape

The most striking thing about the story of Robert Kaufmann is how far away it seems now. It is not just that many people today (though they are in the minority) think that Robert and Walter ought to have been allowed to marry. Rather, even most people who are opposed to same-sex marriage are still willing, as the New York courts in the mid-1960s were not, to allow couples like Robert and Walter to try to create many of the rights of marriage through contracts and wills. Among legal scholars, the *Kaufmann* decision is now widely criticized and discredited.[2]

The shift that has taken place in American culture is most evident in the large number of same-sex couples who indicate that they are openly living together as though they were married, often with children. The 2000 Census found that nearly 600,000 same-sex couples reported themselves as "unmarried partners," compared with 145,130 such households counted by the 1990 Census. The number is probably a substantial undercount because many gay people are unwilling to share this information with the government. Same-sex households were reported in 99.3 percent of U.S. counties in 2000 and were about as racially diverse as the population as a whole. Thirty-four percent of lesbian couples and 22 percent of gay male couples had children. (By comparison, 46 percent of married heterosexual couples were raising children.)[3]

Many opponents of same-sex marriage have argued that same-sex couples can achieve many of the same legal rights as married heterosexual couples through contracts, wills, and powers of attorney. (Although this is true in some cases, what's excluded can be important. For instance, contracts and wills cannot pass on pension rights, nor can they allow a person to inherit a house without having to pay transfer taxes.) This response presupposes that these documents ought to be honored. Liberals and conservatives have moved closer together on these issues.[4]

As this is a book about managing moral disagreement, it makes sense to begin where there is no moral disagreement. It is now generally agreed that homosexual couples have a right to exist, which has implications for the marriage recognition question.

The Kaufmann story also shows how far the nation has moved. As recently as the 1950s, the United States was so far from giving any recognition to same-sex relationships that it devoted substantial law enforcement resources to stamping them out. Gay people were routinely jailed, committed to mental institutions, and randomly beaten, sometimes by the police.[5] All this still sometimes happens, but it is much rarer than it once was.

The Same-Sex Marriage Movement

A newly energized gay liberation movement beginning in the late 1960s challenged this orthodoxy, and recognition of same-sex marriages was one of its first demands. But it quickly became clear that this cause was futile. The first attempts to get courts to declare a right to same-sex marriage took place in the early 1970s, and they were uniformly defeated.[6] The reasoning of these courts was essentially definitional: "Marriage has always been considered as the union of a man and a woman and we have been presented with no authority to the contrary."[7]

Although suits repeatedly were filed throughout the 1980s, these also all lost,[8] and it became the conventional wisdom that such attempts were hopeless. The movement soon shifted its focus to (and enjoyed considerable success with) other issues, such as overturning sodomy laws and combating violence and discrimination.

Gay rights claims of all kinds became more politically potent during the 1980s, largely as a consequence of the willingness of unprecedented numbers of gay people to come out to their friends, families, and coworkers. In 1985, only a quarter of Americans reported having a gay friend, relative, or coworker; in 2000, that proportion had risen to three-quarters of the population. Only a fifth reported not knowing anyone who was gay. The number who reported having a gay friend or close acquaintance grew from 22 percent in 1985 to 56 percent by 2000. Those reporting a gay or lesbian family member rose from 9 percent in 1992 to 23 percent in 2000.[9] Gay people were increasingly visible, and their claims slowly became the claims of familiar human beings, not distant abstractions.

Pressure for recognition of same-sex relationships increased during the 1980s, historian George Chauncey observes, because of the impact of two new developments: the AIDS epidemic and the lesbian baby boom. AIDS victims often had to rely on the assistance of partners who were regarded by the law as legal strangers to them. "Because they were not 'next of kin,'" Chauncey writes, "hospitals could refuse them the right to visit their partners, did not need to consult with them or even inform them about treatment, and could not designate them to sign forms authorizing medical treatments even if they wanted to."[10] Surviving partners sometimes lost their homes when a partner's biological family contested the will or claimed a jointly owned home or property. The willingness of some

courts to set aside wills of gay testators sometimes led partners
to settle for a fraction of their inheritance.

At the same time, increasing numbers of lesbian couples
were having children, typically through the use of donor sperm.
They worried about what would happen if the biological
mother died and a relative contested the right of the surviving
partner to continue to have a relationship with the child. Difficulties also arose when a couple separated. Although both
women had raised the child, the nonbiological mother had no
legal relationship with the child and no right to visitation, and
the biological mother had no claim for child support.

As horror stories accumulated, more couples hired lawyers to prepare wills, medical powers of attorney, and other
documents to provide them with some security. But a complete set of documents approximating the protections of marriage could cost thousands of dollars, more than many couples
could afford. And, as noted earlier, some benefits of marriage
could not be achieved by any contract between the parties. So
gay couples began to campaign for some recognition of their
relationships under the rubric of "domestic partnerships."
Avoiding the term "marriage" made sense because the experience of the 1970s had made it clear that same-sex marriage was
not, even distantly, on the political horizon.

The Shifting Legal Landscape

Gay rights advocates were as surprised as everyone else when a
1993 Hawaii Supreme Court decision seemed to indicate that
that state would shortly have to recognize same-sex marriages.[11]
The court held that the statute discriminated on the basis of
sex and therefore was subject to strict scrutiny under the equal
protection clause of the state constitution. In order to justify

its discrimination against same-sex couples, the court held, the state would have to show that the discrimination is necessary to a compelling state interest. This is a nearly impossible burden to carry, so most observers expected that the state would lose at trial (as in fact it eventually did).[12]

Americans have consistently opposed same-sex marriage by wide margins, so it is not surprising that the reaction to the Hawaii developments in the rest of the United States was strongly negative. In 1996, Congress responded by enacting the federal Defense of Marriage Act (DOMA), which declared that no same-sex marriage would be recognized for federal purposes, such as in filing joint tax returns, awarding social security survivor's benefits, or providing medical insurance for the families of federal employees. The act also indicated that states were not required to recognize marriages from other states when they had strong public policies to the contrary (here basically restating existing law, though with some important and unnoticed modifications).[13] States began enacting their own mini-DOMAs, declaring that they did indeed have public policies against recognizing same-sex marriages valid in other states. As of this writing there are forty such laws on the books. Three other states do not address interstate recognition, but they do have laws denying marriage licenses to same-sex couples.[14]

As it turned out, Hawaii never did recognize same-sex marriage. While the case was still being appealed, a state constitutional amendment was adopted giving the legislature the right to reserve marriage to opposite-sex couples.[15] Other states, however, soon moved toward recognition of same-sex couples. In 1999, the Vermont Supreme Court declared that gay couples were entitled under the state constitution to the same legal rights as married heterosexual couples.[16] The state constitution's "common benefits" clause, which required that government benefits be shared equally by the entire community, required that homosexuals not be excluded from legal benefits and protections available to heterosexuals. The legislature soon responded by enacting a law creating the status of "civil unions," with all the rights of marriage but not the name.[17] In 2003, California did the same thing by statute, calling the relationships "domestic partnerships."[18] (In 2005, the California legislature voted to adopt same-sex marriage, but the bill was vetoed by the governor.) Connecticut passed its own "civil unions" law in 2005.[19] A number of other states offer weaker recognition, with fewer rights.[20] There has been a similar movement in the private sector, as growing numbers of employers provide benefits to employees' same-sex partners.[21]

Same-sex marriage, with the name included, arrived when the Massachusetts Supreme Judicial Court decided in November 2003 that the state constitution was violated by the denial of marriage licenses to gay couples. The court held that there was no rational basis for this discrimination and gave the state six months to comply with its order.[22] It later explained, in response to an inquiry from the legislature, that civil unions were inadequate because they "would have the effect of maintaining and fostering a stigma of exclusion that the Constitution prohibits."[23] Massachusetts started issuing the licenses on May 17, 2004. Officials in some municipalities, notably San Francisco, also issued marriage licenses in defiance of local prohibitions, but these were all soon held to be invalid.

The movement toward same-sex marriage in the 1990s was not confined to the United States. By the time of the Massachusetts decision, same-sex marriage was already legal in the Netherlands, Belgium, and much of Canada.[24] Since then, it has also been legalized in the rest of Canada and in Spain, and as this is written South Africa's Supreme Court has held that it must soon be recognized there as well. (There was some movement in the other direction when Uganda made it a crime to even participate in a private ceremony marrying two people of the same sex.)[25]

Attempts to recognize same-sex marriages generally have been met with countervailing efforts to undo the decisions that created them. Some of these have been limited to defending one's own backyard, while others have been more far-reaching. In Massachusetts, a constitutional amendment banning same-sex marriages and creating civil unions in their place died in the legislature, but another amendment, outlawing both forms of recognition, seems likely to be a ballot initiative in the 2008 election. President George W. Bush endorsed a constitutional amendment banning same-sex marriage throughout the United States, but it failed in both houses of Congress.[26] Another bill, to deny federal courts the right to hear same-sex marriage cases, passed the House but got no further.[27] Many states reinforced their mini-DOMA statutes with amendments to their state constitutions, designed to prevent their state courts from doing what had been done in Massachusetts.

Advocates for same-sex marriage have been arguing that same-sex marriage is a legal right. Their claims rest on four legal arguments:

- People have a fundamental right to marry.
- Discrimination against gays is morally and legally equivalent to discrimination against African-Americans.
- Denial of same-sex marriage is a form of sex discrimination: if Lucy can marry Fred, but Ricky cannot marry Fred, then (assuming that Fred

would be a desirable spouse for either) Ricky is being discriminated against on the basis of his sex.[28]

- Excluding same-sex couples from marriage is unconstitutional because it is just arbitrary and unfair—which is the basis of the decisions in Vermont and Massachusetts.

These arguments have sometimes prevailed in state courts. However, they have consistently failed in the federal courts.[29] The Supreme Court made it clear in its 2003 decision in *Lawrence v. Texas,* which invalidated laws criminalizing homosexual sex, that it has no inclination to go anywhere near the same-sex marriage issue.[30] Even if the Court wanted to impose same-sex marriage, it appears to understand that any such decision would almost certainly be overruled by a constitutional amendment.

Same-sex marriage thus is likely to remain part of the American scene for a long time. As noted above, Massachusetts law cannot change until 2008. No matter what happens there, sooner or later another state will allow same-sex couples to marry. And same-sex marriage continues to exist in all but name in California, Connecticut, and Vermont. Courts have barely begun to sort out what effect Massachusetts marriages will have elsewhere. What will happen if the validity of a same-sex marriage comes into question while a Massachusetts resident is visiting—or moves to—another state? Or when a same-sex spouse from another country comes to the United States?

II

Marriage, Choice of Law, and Public Policy

Shirley Wilkins was sixteen when she decided to marry Stephen Zelichowski. But they had a problem. Under the law of New Jersey, where they both lived, they needed her parents' permission, and her parents evidently were less enthusiastic about Stephen than she was. Shirley and Stephen solved their problem in a creative way. They traveled to Indiana, where the law was less restrictive, got married there, and immediately returned to New Jersey, where they moved in together.

A year later, Shirley had regrets. Stephen, it turned out, was in the habit of stealing cars and was imprisoned on several counts of automobile theft. Shirley wanted to get out of the marriage. If she had married in New Jersey, she would have easily gotten the marriage annulled because she had been underage at the time of the marriage. But the marriage took place in Indiana and was apparently valid under Indiana law.[1]

Annulment was the only way to end the marriage. Under New Jersey law in 1956, when the litigation was taking place, Shirley could not have gotten a divorce. Until 1971, New Jersey allowed divorce only in cases of adultery, desertion, and "extreme cruelty," which was so hard to prove that courts frequently refused to grant divorces even when the husband beat his wife or children or both.[2] So the court had to decide: which state's law applied—New Jersey's or Indiana's? If New Jersey's law applied, she would get her annulment. If Indiana's law applied, she would have to stay married to Stephen.

The New Jersey court gave her the annulment, rejecting what we may call the "blanket rule of recognition"—the idea that, once you're validly married in one state, you're married everywhere.

The case of *Wilkins v. Zelichowski* is an example of a type of legal problem—called *conflict of laws* or *choice of law*—that is familiar to lawyers. This problem arises whenever a dispute involves the laws of more than one jurisdiction, so that the court has to decide which set of laws should be applied. Two people in different states fax to each other their signatures on a contract: which state's contract law governs? Two people from state A get into a car accident in state B. Which state's tort law applies? The rules that govern situations like these are complicated enough that an entire law school course is devoted to covering them.

The problem is not primarily one of constitutional law. The Constitution imposes little constraint on a state's ability to look to its own law when deciding cases in its courts. The constraint, rather, is a common law principle, followed by courts for centuries, of *comity*—respect for the actions of other states.

The core issue in a choice of law case is which state legitimately has the authority to govern the transaction. Choice of law theory has been torn between two ways of approaching this question. Debates about choice of law, Mark Gergen has observed, often implicitly turn "on whether one thinks that state power should be ordered on a territorial or a personal basis. In a territorial order, states have power over events within their borders. In a personal order they have power over events involving their citizens."[3]

For a long time, the territorial approach prevailed in American law. Its classic exposition was the "vested rights" theory developed in the writings of Joseph Beale, reporter for the Restatement (First) of Conflict of Laws, the American Law Institute's authoritative summary of American law, which was published in 1934. Under this approach, a legal right "vests" once the last act that creates a cause of action has occurred. The right thereafter is carried like personal property from one state to another. Thus, for example, if, in a contract negotiation, Ann in Illinois proposes a deal to Betty in New York, and Betty accepts the offer (by either mail or telephone), New York law would apply to the contract because the contract came into existence at the moment when the offer was accepted in New York—the last act that created the contract. If Betty had been in New Jersey when she accepted the offer, then New Jersey law would apply. The law to be applied, regardless of the "forum"—the state where the suit was filed and tried—is the law of the place where the right vested.[4]

Beale's approach has few adherents today (although many states continue to follow the rules he codified). The objection most often raised is that it applies the law of a state that will not experience the consequences of the application of its law. In the example just given, if New Jersey has no other connection with the contract, it makes no sense to apply New Jersey law.

Beale's territorial approach also poses fiendish difficulties of practical workability. Events don't always occur at a single location. Contracts get signed at a single place, but many other occurrences are harder to pinpoint. Suppose a wrongful death case arises in which a person is killed while flying from state A to state B, but the negligent conduct that caused the accident occurred in state C and the plane actually crashed in state D. Or a man slowly eats a box of poisoned candy, piece by piece, while riding a train, becoming sicker and sicker as numerous state lines are crossed, and dying in a state in which he neither received nor ate the poison.

To complicate matters further, in each of the cases just described, it may be relevant whether any of the parties to the litigation are married. In the death cases, someone may or may not have the right to sue, depending on whether he or she were validly married to the person who died. In the contract case, the putative spouse may have inherited rights under the contract.

Under the *vested rights approach,* this determination will have to be made according to the law of the one state in which it is (somehow) found that the transaction occurred or the property is located. Even if predictable rules could be fashioned for making the determination, the results would probably be arbitrary and unfair.

Because of these anomalies, the vested rights approach has been increasingly displaced by what is called *interest analysis,* which tries to balance the legitimate interests—both territorial and personal—of different states in having their own laws apply. Any choice of law rule implies certain premises about political legitimacy.[5] It decides the limits of each state's right to rule the world. If a state's law is appropriately applied to a transaction, it must be because the state has a legitimate right to govern that transaction.

Two such premises about legitimacy are relevant to the same-sex marriage question. The first is that states have a right to decide what will happen within their borders. This is the basis of the territorial approach. The second is that states can exercise political authority over their citizens. This is the basis of the personal approach. Each can be a legitimate basis for authority. Even visitors to a state have to obey its laws while they are there. And your home jurisdiction may have a right to govern your behavior even when you travel.[6] The United States, for example, has recently made it a crime for American citizens to have sex with children while they are traveling abroad.[7]

What makes the choice of law problem so difficult with respect to marriage questions is that both territorial and personal considerations are in play. A territorial approach to marriage could say in the *Wilkins* case that Indiana law applies because the marriage took place there, or that New Jersey law applies because that is where the relationship is actually located. A personal approach could say that Indiana law applies because the couple was present there, or that New Jersey law applies because they were citizens of New Jersey.[8] If one takes a step back and looks at each state's interest in applying its own marriage laws to its own citizens, then there is still a tension. In the same-sex marriage case, it is as important for Massachusetts to be able to say that its citizens *can* marry others of the same sex as it is for Utah or Wyoming, for instance, to be able to say that its citizens *cannot* do so.

And, if one is balancing interests, there are individual interests that should also be taken into account. The balancing of interests across different jurisdictions should not make it impossible for the people involved to know whether they are married, and it should not arbitrarily disrupt their relationships. "Because marriage is a continuing relationship," a leading conflicts treatise observes, "there is normally a need that its existence be subject to regulation by one law without occasion for repeated redetermination of the validity."[9] With the advent of the automobile and the airplane, many people cross state lines every day, often on their way to and from their jobs. It would be ridiculous to have people's marital status blink on and off like a strobe light as they jet across the country.

Before the same-sex marriage controversy arose, American law had arrived at a fairly simple rule for accommodating all these interests in marriage recognition cases. This is how it is stated in the Restatement (Second) of Conflict of Laws, the successor to Beale's work, which was published in 1971: "A marriage which satisfies the requirements of the state where the marriage was contracted will everywhere be recognized as valid unless it violates the strong public policy of another state which had the most significant relationship to the spouses and the marriage at the time of the marriage."[10]

The general contours of the rule should be familiar. Once you're married in one state, you're married. But there is an exception if a state has a closer relationship to the parties than the place where the marriage is celebrated and that state has a strong public policy against the marriage. Generally, the place with the "most significant relationship" will be the state where the couple makes their home.[11]

On the basis of this kind of exception, the New Jersey courts had no difficulty annulling Shirley Wilkins's marriage. Indiana had no relationship to the spouses; they were only there for a day. New Jersey, on the other hand, had enacted its nonage law precisely to protect its young people from the kind of mistake that Shirley had made. The state supreme court wrote that "it seems clear to us that if New Jersey's public policy is to remain at all meaningful it must be considered equally applicable though their marriage took place in Indiana." The only interested state was New Jersey because "both parties were domiciled in New Jersey before and after the marriage and their matrimonial domicile was established here."[12]

The basic idea is that each state governs its own citizens. And this means that each state gets to decide who its own citizens can marry. If your home is New Jersey, then New Jersey law determines who you can marry. Indiana can allow sixteen-year-olds to marry, but they'd better be from Indiana or from some other state that allows them to marry. Indiana has no legitimate interest in thwarting the operation of New Jersey law.

However, notice the limits of New Jersey's power here. Under the Restatement rule, New Jersey gets to invoke its public policy if the parties live in New Jersey *at the time of the marriage.* Once a pair of sixteen-year-olds marry in Indiana, they can afterward migrate to New Jersey, and New Jersey will have to recognize their marriage even if they haven't turned eighteen yet.

The Restatement offers the prevailing way of balancing state interests concerning marriage recognition. It allows states to enforce their public policies at the time of the marriage, but if the marriage is valid where it is celebrated, it is valid everywhere. This rule would offer us a quick and clean solution to the same-sex marriage question. Only residents of Massachusetts would be permitted to enter into same-sex marriages. Once they were married, they could migrate anywhere in the United States. And once they got to their new home—say, Utah—that state would have to recognize the marriage.

These cases would turn, then, on where the parties are domiciled. This is not unusual in choice of law cases. The domicile of one of the parties is often crucial in choice of law decisions. The place of one's domicile can tax one's income and estate, and also determines, if one dies without a will, which state's law of intestate succession applies. A person can always be sued in a court of his or her domicile.

But domicile is not always easy to discern. The general rule is that *a person's domicile is the place where he or she makes his or her home and intends to remain.* Intention, then, is crucial to the question of whether someone has changed domicile. The classic illustration is the case of *White v. Tennant.*[13] Michael White, who had lived all his life in West Virginia, sold his farm and moved to a new farm, which straddled the West Virginia/Pennsylvania border. He arrived at the new house in Pennsylvania, but his wife became ill, and so that same day the couple went a few hundred yards back to the family home in West Virginia. Michael himself then became ill and died two weeks later. West Virginia and Pennsylvania had different rules for intestate succession. Michael was found to be a Pennsylvania domiciliary. He had abandoned his West Virginia home with no intention of returning, and so Pennsylvania became his domicile the moment he set foot there. His immediate return to West Virginia was irrelevant because he did not intend to reestablish a home in West Virginia. His intentions determined the outcome of the case.

It is not always easy to know what someone intends. Shirley Wilkins and Stephen Zelichowski left Indiana as soon as they were married. There was no ambiguity about their intentions. Suppose, however, that they had stayed there for three months? Six months? How could a court be sure whether they intended to remain in Indiana? Problems of this kind led

Supreme Court Justice Joseph Story, in his 1834 treatise on conflict of laws, to endorse a blanket rule validating all such marriages, even in evasion cases. It is, he wrote, "far better to support marriages celebrated in a foreign country as valid, when in conformity with the laws of that country, although the rule may produce some minor inconveniences, than, by introducing distinctions as to the designs and objects and motives of the parties, to shake the general confidence in such marriages, to subject the innocent issue to constant doubts as to their own legitimacy, and to leave the parents themselves to cut adrift from their solemn obligations when they may become discontented with their lot."[14]

The obvious trouble with the Restatement rule, in the context of same-sex marriage, is that Utah, for instance, has a very strong public policy against recognizing same-sex marriages, and its policy is as much violated by a migrant gay couple setting up housekeeping in Salt Lake City as it is by a local couple doing so after a weekend trip to Boston. Any solution needs to give appropriate weight to that policy. It would also be strange for recent immigrants to Utah to have an entitlement to same-sex marriage that is denied to longtime residents.

The Public Policy Doctrine

The rule that generally validates marriage, we have seen, is subject to an exception based on public policy. What is this public policy doctrine? Once we have determined its general meaning, we will be able to figure out how and to what extent it can legitimately be applied to the question of when to recognize same-sex marriages.

Here is how the rule is stated in one conflicts treatise: "Invoking the concept of 'public policy,' a court can refuse to enforce, as contrary to its own notions of justice and fairness, a rule found in the state designated by the forum's choice-of-law rule."[15] In a situation in which a state would ordinarily apply another forum's law, in other words, the public policy doctrine permits the state nonetheless to prefer its own law.

The public policy doctrine, then, is not unique to marriage law; it can be invoked wherever a court has to decide an issue of conflict of laws. It dates back to the Middle Ages, when medieval authorities talked about "odious statutes" whose territorial reach should be circumscribed narrowly.[16] The doctrine was employed in Anglo-Saxon law as early as the fifteenth century.[17]

Courts have struggled to define the conditions that trigger the public policy rule. Some courts have formulated the doctrine so broadly that it would crowd out all foreign law altogether. (In choice of law, "foreign" means the law of any jurisdiction other than the forum, meaning other states as well as other countries.) Thus, for example, the New York Court of Appeals once justified the application of one of its own rules to a transaction that had occurred in Connecticut with the argument that "a state can have no public policy except what is to be found in its Constitution and laws."[18] Professor Russell Weintraub observes that this definition of public policy "was so parochial that, if applied literally, all conflicts analysis would be ended. No foreign rule that differed from local law could be applied at the forum."[19] Other courts held that suit would not be allowed if the foreign statute were "substantially dissimilar" to the one at the forum dealing with the same matter. This rule never made much sense, and little remains of it today.[20]

Perhaps because the public policy doctrine has the potential to displace all other choice of law rules, it is not often invoked. Modern commentators warn against its too-frequent use.[21] In Judge (later Supreme Court Justice) Benjamin Cardozo's classic formulation, courts should not refuse to entertain a foreign cause of action unless application of the foreign law "would violate some fundamental principle of justice, some prevalent conception of good morals, some deep-rooted tradition of the common weal."[22]

What sense does the public policy doctrine make? For much of the twentieth century, it has been the subject of vigorous attack, particularly with respect to cases in which the foreign law was that of another state. The principal objection that has been raised is that the doctrine was needlessly parochial. John Beach observed in 1918 that the public policy doctrine had been invoked in cases involving such trivia as "the propriety of dealings in cotton futures, or speculations in stocks on margin, or stipulations exempting telegraph companies from liability for negligence in the transmission and delivery of unrepeated telegrams."[23] The doctrine's critics had little difficulty finding cases in which it had been invoked that, in retrospect, looked ridiculous. In 1933, one writer noted that four decades earlier, "dealing in futures was denominated a 'dangerous evil,' a 'vice'; not only against public policy, but a crime against the state, religion, morality, and legitimate trades and businesses, a 'blighting curse.' Transactions of this sort have since become almost indispensable to the credit structure of the country."[24]

Two defenses were offered in response to this objection. The first of these, which I'll call the *legitimate-interest rationale*, argued that the public policy doctrine is in practice typically used, not in order to assert the forum's control over a situation entirely foreign to its concerns, but only to vindicate the state's own legitimate interests.[25] The most sophisticated presentation of this argument, offered in 1956 by Professors Monrad Paulsen and Michael Sovern, surveyed the cases in which public policy had been relied on and found that in nearly all of them the forum had some important connection with the underlying transaction, which made it fair for the forum to apply its own law.[26] What the rule was really rejecting was the rigidity of the vested rights approach. It was applying a kind of incipient interest analysis.

The second defense of the public policy doctrine is that some foreign laws are so dreadful that they ought not to be enforced. I will call this the *repugnance rationale*. Thus, one early court explained that in choosing the applicable law, courts should not "exhibit to the citizens of the state an example pernicious and detestable."[27] In order for this rationale to apply, the underlying law must be pretty extreme. Some courts held that, in order for otherwise applicable foreign law to be disregarded under the public policy doctrine, "we must be able to find but one pervading feeling upon that subject,—so much so, that a contrary feeling, in an individual, would denominate him either insane, or diseased in his moral perceptions."[28] Modern commentators have agreed that some laws cross this threshold.[29] One judge declared that American courts should not "be required to recognize and enforce in our courts the racial laws of South Africa [this was in 1985], the religious laws of Iran and the sexually discriminatory laws of Saudi Arabia."[30]

This defense of the doctrine is frankly parochial: your law is so bad, and our law is so much better, that we will disregard yours at every opportunity. The repugnance rationale thus has the character of a sort of declaration of judicial war on the foreign state. It indicates, in effect, that the foreign law will be treated as no law at all because it ought not to exist at all. Parties are invited to come to the forum with their claims, for the obnoxious foreign law (which presumably operates adversely to those claims) will be ignored, and to that extent undermined. Such declarations are sometimes justified. For example, it should not have been a defense to a lawsuit for breach of contract that because a party was a Jew, a corporation was authorized by Nazi Germany's laws to break an agreement with him.[31]

The legitimate-interest rationale explains the invocation of public policy in cases like *Wilkins*. Only New Jersey had a legitimate interest in Shirley Wilkins's marriage. The premise about political legitimacy is straightforward. As the Supreme Court put it in 1942, "[e]ach state as a sovereign has a rightful and legitimate concern in the marital status of persons domiciled within its borders."[32] New Jersey wasn't trying to interfere with any other state's effort to determine the marital status of that state's own residents.

Since each state regulates marriages within its borders, no state ought to have to automatically defer to marriages of its own domiciliaries in another state because those are marriages in which the foreign state has no legitimate interest. This is why the result in the *Wilkins* case made sense. If New Jersey could legitimately determine that its residents must be eighteen years old in order to marry, then it was ridiculous to allow this policy to be evaded by the insipid device of driving across the border and spending an hour in another state with a lower age of consent.[33]

If any particular state's marriage restrictions unduly infringe the liberty of its citizens, then the restriction ought to be discarded wholesale for that reason, not evaded piecemeal by tricks. If same-sex couples are entitled to marry, that right should not be conditional on the ability to afford airplane tickets to Boston, however much this might help tourism there. If, as many think, there is to be a national right to same-sex marriage, it should be because no state has the power to deny such marriages, regardless of the actions of other states.

The repugnance rationale for the public policy exception is more far-reaching than the legitimate-interest rationale because it extends to transactions with which the forum has no connection other than the accident of being the place of trial.[34] It makes no sense in the federal system. Particularly now that the federal courts increasingly police the states to make sure they comply with national norms, there is no legitimate place for states condemning as repugnant one another's laws. It is notable that as long ago as 1940, one commentator defending the public policy doctrine found it necessary to note that "fascist tendencies have temporarily prevailed in one state."[35] Presumably he was writing about Louisiana under the Earl Long political machine (inherited from Earl's more famous brother, Huey). No state today is in that bad a condition. A state may legitimately assert its right to govern itself as it sees fit. It may occasionally pronounce odious and unenforceable the law of foreign tyrannies. What it may not do is denounce and attempt to disrupt other states' efforts to govern themselves.[36]

The application of the repugnance rationale is contrary to the rule of law. This is because it invites "forum-shopping," the stratagem in which someone who is about to file a suit picks a court that is likely to rule in his or her favor. Under the repugnance rationale, the forum state will impose its own rule even if another state has a greater interest in regulating the transaction and so would have the stronger claim to have its law apply.

Douglas Laycock has observed that any choice of law rule that permits the forum to prefer its own law, just because it is its own, is irreconcilable with basic principles of federalism. In a federal system, no state can have a legitimate interest in deliberately subverting the operation of the laws of other states. Under any rule that automatically prefers the forum's law, Laycock observes, "no person can know the law that governs his conduct until after his case has been decided."[37] But an essential element of the rule of law is that people should be able to identify, before they act, the rules that will be applied to their conduct.

Uncertainty in the area of marriage is about as intolerable as it is in any area of the law. "If there is one thing that the people are entitled to expect from their lawmakers," Supreme Court Justice Robert Jackson wrote in 1948, "it is rules of law that will enable individuals to tell whether they are married and, if so, to whom."[38] Therefore, any choice of law principle, to be acceptable, must set forth a uniform rule that can be followed by all states that apply the law. Since the repugnance rationale for the public policy rule makes uniformity impossible, it can have no legitimate place in interstate choice of law decisions, such as whether to recognize a marriage valid in another state.

Making Public Policy Definite

Public policy is sometimes said to be an amorphous and unpredictable doctrine. Over time, however, it needn't be. Even the vaguest judicial standard becomes clearer as a body of decided cases comes to encrust its surface. It is possible for a court, deciding whether to apply public policy, to be guided by past cases in which similar conflicts situations arose. Most relevantly here, if in an earlier case there was a public policy that was at least as strong as the public policy at issue in today's case, and if in the earlier case the public policy exception was *not* invoked, then a court should conclude that the exception should not be invoked in the instant case.

In order to develop a more nuanced understanding of the public policy doctrine and how it might appropriately operate today, we are going to have to look at the law of an earlier time. This is not the first time that states were bitterly divided about what kinds of marriage were legitimate. The exercise is going to feel peculiar because we are going to have to treat policies as substantial that we now regard as worthless and even evil. But a well-developed body of law is there that offers us the beginnings of a solution to our present problem. We would be foolish not to consider what it might have to teach us.

III

Miscegenation in the Conflict of Laws

In May 1873, Sarah Spake left her home in North Carolina and crossed the border into South Carolina. There she married Pink Ross. Sarah was white; Pink was black. They would have been barred from marrying in North Carolina, but at that time, South Carolina, although it had been part of the Confederacy, had no law against interracial marriage. Northern troops continued to occupy the South in the wake of the Civil War, and the supporters of white supremacy were in retreat, although they would seize power again in a few years.

Within a few months, Sarah and Pink decided to move to North Carolina. They traveled there in August and settled in Charlotte. Three years later they were arrested for fornication. They admitted their cohabitation but defended against the charge by arguing that they were lawfully married. The state responded that their marriage was void in North Carolina.

The trial judge dismissed the charge, and a divided state supreme court agreed. The court rejected the state's claim that

Sarah had sought to evade the law. There was no evidence that, when she married Pink, she had intended ever to return to North Carolina: "It is difficult to see how in going to South Carolina to marry a negro, without an intent to return with him to this State, she could evade or intend to evade the laws of this State. Our laws have no extra territorial operation, and do not attempt to prohibit the marriage in South Carolina of blacks and whites domiciled in that State."[1]

The court was eager to make clear that it did not condone interracial marriage. It said that such marriages were "revolting to us and to all persons, who, by reason of living in States where the two races are nearly equal in numbers, have an experience of the consequences of matrimonial connections between them."[2] This was not, however, "the common sentiment of the civilized and Christian world":[3] "The general rule is admitted that a marriage between citizens of a foreign State contracted in that State and valid by its laws is valid everywhere where the parties might migrate, although not contracted with the rites required by the law of the country into which they come and between persons disqualified by such law from intermarrying."[4]

Because of the strong common interest in uniformity, marriages not deemed odious to all had to be given extraterritorial recognition by all. "Upon this question above all others it is desirable . . . that there should not be one law in Maine and another in Texas, but that the same law shall prevail at least throughout the United States."[5] Because the civilized world was not united in rejecting interracial marriages, North Carolina had a duty to join the rest of civilization in enforcing the common rule. "The law of nations is a part of the law of North Carolina. We are under obligations of comity to our sister States."[6]

Two judges dissented, insisting on the forum state's right to govern within its territory: "If such a marriage solemnized here between our own people is declared void, why should comity require the evil to be imported from another State? Why is not the relation severed the instant they set foot upon our soil?"[7] If this consequence is inconvenient to some, "individuals who have formed relations which are obnoxious to our laws can find their comfort in staying away from us."[8] In coming to North Carolina and asking that their marriage be recognized, the dissent argued, the defendants were asking for more than that to which North Carolina's own citizens were entitled: "It is courteous for neighbors to visit, and it is handsome to allow the visitor family privileges and even give him the favorite seat; but if he bring his pet rattlesnake or his pet bear or spitz dog, famous for hydrophobia, he must leave them outside the door. And if he bring smallpox the door may be shut against him."[9]

The division within the court shows us that the passions associated with the same-sex marriage question are hardly unprecedented. Same-sex marriage may appear to be a novel legal issue, but deep moral divisions over marriage are not at all novel. They have been with us before, and courts' efforts to address them in the past can teach us something now.

Polygamy, Incest, Miscegenation

The public policy exception has been invoked primarily in three contexts: polygamy, incest, and interracial marriage, or miscegenation.[10] The first two were misnomers to some extent.

The only jurisdictions in which polygamy was ever legally valid in the United States were certain Native American reservations, and when such practices were questioned in litigation, the attitude of state courts was uniformly one of "casual tolerance."[11] No state ever legalized polygamy.

Polygamy was, of course, common among the Mormons for a long time, and it survives in some rural communities. But the Mormons didn't feel the need to have the state recognize their unions. Since the Mormons first arrived in Utah, the governing law was always either that of Mexico or the common law of Great Britain, neither of which recognized polygamous marriages. The Mormon Church did have an elaborate system of ecclesiastical courts, which often adjudicated domestic relations disputes involving polygamous marriages. These courts, however, did not issue decisions that the state would enforce, and their authority was not recognized by the civil courts for any purpose. The only sanction the church courts had—but it could be a potent one—was the power to withhold fellowship from (meaning in practice, to ostracize in the community) anyone who refused to comply with their commands.[12] So polygamy was never recognized as part of the positive law of any jurisdiction in the United States, not even Utah when it was under Mormon control, and no conflict of laws problem ever arose in connection with American polygamy.[13]

Most "polygamy" cases involved subsequent marriages of parties who had obtained divorces, at a time when divorced people were often forbidden to remarry. (Such restrictions were most often imposed on a former spouse who, the court had found, had committed adultery.)[14] Such restrictions have now become obsolete, but while they were in effect courts were divided about how to treat remarriages in other states, with the weight of authority tending to favor recognition of the second marriage.[15] Cases did occasionally arise involving polygamous or potentially polygamous marriages contracted abroad. With few exceptions,[16] courts recognized these marriages.[17] The blanket rule of nonrecognition never prevailed with respect to polygamous marriages.

Similarly, no state ever violated the core instances of the incest taboo by legalizing parent-child or sibling marriages. The incest cases involved marriages between first cousins, aunts and nephews, uncles and nieces, or even more remote relations. Although earlier cases tended to invalidate such marriages, later ones have tended to uphold them.[18] Even the most hostile of the earlier cases, which sustained criminal prosecution of an uncle who had married his niece, relied primarily on the fact that the prohibited incestuous conduct had occurred on the soil of the forum and reasoned that the forum therefore had a sufficient reason to look to its own criminal law.[19]

Interracial marriage aroused the strongest passions in the courts. Miscegenation prohibitions were in force as early as the 1660s, but only after the Civil War did they begin to function as a central sanction in the system of white supremacy. At one time or another, forty-one American colonies and states enacted laws against interracial marriage. In 1967, the Supreme Court declared unconstitutional every miscegenation prohibition in the country, thereby eliminating any conflict of laws with respect to this issue.[20]

The Functions of the Miscegenation Taboo

The miscegenation taboo was held in the southern states with great tenacity; it was an important part of American racism.[21] Such marriages were rare, but enormous energies were expended in preventing them from occurring.

The taboo had multiple functions, and so it served multiple state interests. First and foremost, it was necessary to the maintenance of racial caste. In the patriarchal society of early America, children ordinarily inherited the status of their fathers. This meant that children begotten by male slaveowners upon female slaves (most interracial sex, even in the early colonies, followed this pattern) would be free and would have a claim for support from their fathers.[22] With interracial sex outlawed, children inherited the slave status of their mothers, and the social order was preserved.[23] The prohibition in practice also helped to maintain gender hierarchy, by preserving white males' exclusive access to white women while ignoring their liaisons with black women.

The prohibition also had a psychological function. The identity of southern whites was defined at a fundamental level by their status as white, as contrasted with the purported laziness, stupidity, uncleanliness, criminal propensity, and hypersexuality of blacks. The miscegenation taboo appears to be close to the psychological core of the system of white supremacy that prevailed in the South after Reconstruction.[24] Its prototypical mode of enforcement was the lynch mob.[25] As Joel Kovel observes, "the archetypal lynching in the old South was for the archetypal crime of having a black man rape (= touch, approach, look at, be imagined to have looked at, talk back to, etc.) a white lady."[26] White supremacy was thus understood, and often expressly justified, as a means of protecting white women from black men.[27] The taboo was deeply rooted in culturally shared aversions that even strong antiracists usually could not escape internalizing. Harry Truman, who nearly lost the presidency in 1948 because of his dedication to the ideal of racial equality, said in 1963: "I don't believe in it. What's that word about ten feet long? Miscegenation? Would you want your daughter to marry a Negro?"[28]

Many writers have explored the psychological basis of this understanding (which needed explaining; one writer observed that the actual danger that a southern white woman would be raped by a black man was much less than her danger of being struck by lightning[29]), and they have arrived at widely divergent conclusions.[30] Most promising is the hypothesis that some kind of projected guilt was at work. John Dollard thought that "the white men are defending their women not only from the sexual thoughts and attentions of Negroes, but also from their own, and what they deny to themselves in fantasy they will hardly permit Negroes in fact."[31] Calvin Hernton argues that there were two sources of such guilt for the southern white man: his frequent cohabitation with black women, and his sense of the immorality of slavery, and later, of the Jim Crow system.[32] White womanhood was perceived as precious but endangered, and this danger justified all the repressive measures that were brought to bear on the black population. In Kovel's Freudian account, the black man became the surrogate for the white man's own oedipal fears: the white man simultaneously became the feared castrating father and the son who in turn overcomes and castrates the father.[33]

It's hard to be confident of any psychological account because the underlying processes cannot be observed. It is clear, however, that the taboo evoked emotions of astonishing power.

Perhaps the most thoroughly documented lynching is the murder of Emmett Till. Till, a fourteen-year-old boy visiting relatives in Mississippi in 1955, made a leering remark at a white woman in a store. A few days later, the woman's husband and brother kidnapped, beat, shot, and mutilated him. The police refused to do any investigative work to help the prosecution. A special prosecutor had to be appointed, and he was given no budget or staff. Prominent attorneys volunteered to represent the accused, and a defense fund raised ten thousand dollars. The murderers were identified in court by eyewitnesses, but they were quickly acquitted by an all-white, all-male jury. The witnesses had to leave town for their own safety.[34] The entire white community evidently agreed that the barest hint of interracial sex was sufficient provocation to justify the torture and murder of a child.

The caste-preserving and psychological functions of the miscegenation taboo converged to support a third function: that of consolidating white political support for the system of white supremacy after the Civil War. The fear of miscegenation became a basis for resisting movements for civil rights, women's rights, and, crucially, the Populist movement of the late nineteenth century, which for a brief time united poor blacks and whites against wealthy landowners and creditors. Poor white men were persuaded that the protection of their prerogatives as white males took precedence over other concerns. The fear of rape by black men helped to induce white women to submit to the protection of white men. The psychological power of the miscegenation taboo was sufficient to override class interests and egalitarian ideals. It became the keystone of the whole political system.

These were, in short, not trivial state interests. They were central to the sociopolitical system of the South for nearly a century after the Civil War and Reconstruction.

These state interests are, of course, evil ones, and there is something grotesque about a legal system solemnly honoring them in this way. Yet it is revealing that even here, in this fundamentally vicious and pitiless system, the interest in marriage recognition was given some weight.

The Legal Prohibition

As one might expect, when the southern courts defended the prohibition, they were at least as passionate in their denunciations as the modern opponents of same-sex marriage are. In

1878 a Virginia court wrote: "The purity of public morals, the moral and physical development of both races, and the highest advancement of our cherished southern civilization, under which two distinct races are to work out and accomplish the destiny to which the Almighty has assigned them on this continent—all require that they should be kept distinct and separate, and that connections and alliances so unnatural that God and nature seem to forbid them, should be prohibited by positive law, and be subject to no evasion."[35]

The southern states typically went far beyond the recent legislation prohibiting same-sex marriage by making interracial marriage a felony. And often it was specifically *marriage,* and not merely interracial sex, that was criminalized. In some states, it was necessary to prove cohabitation in order to convict for miscegenation;[36] in others, the prosecutor was required to prove an actual marriage.[37] One conviction was reversed because, although the ceremony had taken place, the officiating notary's commission had expired![38] It would, in short, be hard to argue that the southern states' public policy against miscegenation was *less* strong than modern public policies against same-sex marriage.

Yet even in this charged context, the southern states did not make a blunderbuss of their own public policy. Their decisions concerning the validity of interracial marriages were surprisingly fact-dependent. They did not utterly disregard the interests of the parties to the forbidden marriages or of the states that had recognized such marriages, but weighed these against the countervailing interests of the forum. Where the forum's interests were attenuated, southern courts sometimes upheld marriages between blacks and whites.

Three classes of choice of law problems arose involving interracial marriages. Two of these were easily resolved. The third was harder.

In the first category—call them the *evasion cases*—were cases in which parties had traveled out of their home state for the express purpose of evading that state's prohibition of their marriages, and thereafter immediately returned home. Southern courts always invalidated these marriages.

Second were *extraterritorial cases* in which the parties had never lived within the state, but in which the marriage was relevant to litigation conducted there. Typically, after the death of one spouse, the other sought to inherit property that was located within the forum state. In these cases, even in the most racist states, the courts always recognized the marriages.

The final category was the *migratory case* in which the parties had contracted a marriage valid where they lived and subsequently moved to a state where interracial marriages were prohibited—without ever intending to evade the law. These were the most difficult cases, and the southern authorities were divided on how to deal with them.

The Evasion Cases

Edmund Kinney, who was black, married Mary S. Hall, who was white, in October 1878 in Washington, D.C. They both were from Virginia, and after their short trip together to Washington, they returned home. Earlier that year, Virginia had passed a law criminalizing interracial marriage. Both were convicted and sentenced to the maximum of five years at hard labor.

Edmund petitioned the federal district court for a writ of habeas corpus. He claimed that the Constitution held "that a marriage lawful in the District of Columbia is lawful everywhere in the United States." The court rejected the claim, holding that the marriage was a fraud on the laws of Virginia. Edmund brought back with him to Virginia "no other right in regard to the marriage which he made abroad than he took

away. He cannot bring the marriage privileges of a citizen of
the District of Columbia any more than he could those of a citizen of Utah, into Virginia, in violation of her laws."[39] Edmund
and Mary served out their sentences in Virginia's prisons.[40]

Nearly every court that addressed the issue came to the
same conclusion.[41] As far as they were concerned, this was just
like the *Wilkins* case considered in Chapter 2, in which New
Jersey refused to honor the marriage of a sixteen-year-old who
had briefly traveled to another state to marry. The logic was the
same in both cases. If a state's public policy is worth having
at all, then it makes no sense to allow it to be circumvented
so easily.

Even here, however, courts were not unanimous. The earliest case involving an attempt to evade a prohibition on interracial marriage, *Medway v. Needham*,[42] arose in Massachusetts
in 1819. A mulatto man and a white woman, both domiciled in
Massachusetts, had gone to Rhode Island, where interracial
marriage was legal, in order to escape their home state's prohibition of their marriage. The court upheld the marriage,
emphasizing, as modern authorities do, the importance of cer-
tainty and uniformity with respect to the existence of a marriage. A contrary rule would involve "extreme inconveniences
and cruelty";[43] the rule it adopted "must be founded on principles of policy, with a view to prevent the disastrous consequences to the issue of such marriages, as well as to avoid the
public mischief, which would result from the loose state, in
which people so situated would live."[44] The court acknowl-
edged that there would have to be limits to its holding: "If
without any restriction, then it might be that incestuous marriages might be contracted between citizens of a state where
they were held unlawful and void, in countries where they
were not prohibited; and the parties return to live in defiance

of the religion and laws of their own country. But it is not to be inferred from a toleration of marriages which are prohibited merely on account of political expediency, that others, which would tend to outrage principles and feelings of all civilized nations, would be countenanced."[45]

The leading American treatise on conflict of laws defended the result in *Medway*,[46] but it was criticized by others,[47] was never followed in any miscegenation case,[48] and was later overruled by a marriage evasion statute.[49]

The Extraterritorial Cases

Cases sometimes arose in which a marriage came into issue after one of the spouses had died without a will, and the other sought to inherit some property located in the state. Courts routinely upheld the marriages in these cases. They reasoned that, because the purpose of the law was to prevent interracial couples from living together within the state's borders, there would be no harm in recognizing the marriage after the death of one partner and consequently allowing the surviving spouse or (thereby legitimated) children to inherit the decedent's property. All deemed it dispositive that their states' laws were not intended to have any extraterritorial application.

A telling example comes from Mississippi in 1948—one of the worst periods in one of the nastiest bastions of segregation in the United States. In 1923, Pearl Mitchell, who was black, and Alex Miller, who was white, were indicted in Hinds County, Mississippi, for unlawful cohabitation. The district attorney agreed not to pursue the charges if the couple would leave the state, and so they moved to Chicago. They lived together for a number of years and married in 1939. Six years later, Pearl died without a will, leaving land that she had owned in Mississippi. Pearl's relatives and Alex both claimed the land. The relatives, relying on a provision in the state constitution that declared interracial marriages "unlawful and void," claimed that such a marriage could not be recognized for any purpose in Mississippi. The Mississippi Supreme Court, however, decided that in this context, the marriage was valid. "The manifest and recognized purpose of this statute was to prevent persons of Negro and white blood from living together in this state in the relationship of husband and wife," the court explained in *Miller v. Lucks.* "What we are requested to do is simply to recognize this marriage to the extent only of permitting one of the parties thereto to inherit from the other property in Mississippi, and to that extent it must and will be recognized."[50]

The same result was reached in earlier cases. A Spaniard named Caballero came to New Orleans in 1832 and became a U.S. citizen. While there, he lived with a colored woman named Carolina Visinier, who bore him several children. He returned to Spain in 1856. On the way, he stopped in Havana, where he married Carolina. He stayed in Spain for three years and then returned to New Orleans, where he died in 1866. Thereafter, his daughter, a Mrs. Conte, sued for a share of the estate, which the executor resisted on the grounds that the interracial marriage was void. The executor noted that Louisiana's Civil Code declared interracial marriages "forbidden," "void," and a "nullity." The Supreme Court of Louisiana held that Mrs. Conte could inherit. The prohibition of interracial marriage, the court explained, "was of local and limited effect. It existed for a purpose local and special in this country. That purpose could not have been more effectually carried out by withholding from persons abroad, legitimate by the laws of the country where they lived, the right of inheriting property in this State."[51]

A similar case arose, and was resolved in the same way, in Florida in 1913. Elizabeth Anderson, who "had one-eighth or more of negro blood in her veins," owned a lot in Pensacola, Florida, which she continued to own after she moved to Leavenworth, Kansas, where she married a white man named W. J. Grooms. After she died (without a will), Grooms sold the lot to R. E. L. McCaskill. Elizabeth's mother, Josephine Whittington, then challenged the sale and sought to recover the lot. She claimed that, since the Florida constitution declared interracial marriages "forever prohibited" and a state statute deemed them "utterly null and void," Grooms could not inherit Elizabeth's Florida property. The Supreme Court of Florida disagreed: "Since the marriage was valid in the state of Kansas, where it was consummated and where the parties continued to reside until the death of the wife, we are of the opinion that neither our constitution nor the statutes . . . have any applicability thereto."[52]

To see how extreme the application of the prohibition to extraterritorial cases would be, we must turn to comparative law. Outside of the United States, there have been only two well-developed bodies of racist law: apartheid South Africa and Nazi Germany. While these regimes did try to restrict some extraterritorial marriages, even they did not seek to extend their marriage prohibitions beyond their own nationals.

South Africa's 1949 Prohibition of Mixed Marriages Act prohibited its male citizens or domiciliaries from entering an interracial marriage in another country. It did not apply to foreigners or to South Africans who emigrated and changed citizenship.[53] Like the Jim Crow South, South Africa did not seek to apply its law outside its borders; the law's preeminent object appears to have been, once more, the prevention of interracial cohabitation within the country.[54]

Unsurprisingly, the prohibition of interracial marriage that was least respectful of territorial boundaries was that of Nazi Germany. (Here our working assumption, that the jurisdictions we have been considering have no desire to rule the world, would obviously be misplaced.) The Law for the Protection of German Blood and Honor, one of the infamous Nuremberg Laws of 1935, declared that "marriages between Jews and nationals of German or kindred blood are forbidden" and that such marriages were void and criminal "even if, for the purpose of evading this law, they are concluded abroad."[55] A German court applied the law to sustain a prosecution where a couple had traveled to Switzerland to marry, intending never to return to Germany. The intent to remain outside Germany was irrelevant, the court held, because in view of the laws of the Nazi regime, that is what generally happens, and so to consider it would always negate an intent to evade, thus making the law ineffectual.[56] Even after this case, however, the courts of Nazi Germany were willing to give full extraterritorial effect to German criminal laws only in cases where the accused was a German national, ordinarily resident in Germany, who went outside Germany in order to evade German law; the act affected vital German interests; and "the sound instinct of the people regarded the act as committed in Germany or as equal to an act committed in Germany."[57] This is not an example that any state should want to emulate.

The Migratory Cases

If marriages are void if, at the time of the marriage, the parties are trying to evade their home state's restriction, then once a couple is legitimately married according to the law of the state where they make their home, they should be able to move anywhere and take their marriage with them. This is the Restatement (Second) rule, discussed in Chapter 2, and this is what the North Carolina court held in the case of *State v. Ross* described at the beginning of this chapter. But it is easy to see why the southern states resisted this solution.

One obvious difficulty with drawing the lines in this way was that, as we saw in the last chapter, a marriage would be valid or not depending on whether the parties, at the time of the marriage, intended to return to the domicile that prohibited their marriage. And it can be hard to tell what someone intended, particularly when the question arises years after the marriage. But the more forceful objection was that articulated by the *Ross* dissenters. Recognition in migratory cases would mean that the southern states would have to tolerate some interracial cohabitation within their borders after all. Only two state statutes spoke to the issue, and only four cases arose in which an interracial couple had moved to the forum state. One of the statutes clearly permitted migratory marriages, and the other was ambiguous but quite possibly did so. In each of the four cases, either the marriages were recognized or the scope of the nonrecognition was uncertain.

A 1906 Louisiana miscegenation statute imposed criminal penalties on "any person, domiciled in this State, between whom marriage is prohibited . . . who shall leave this State for the purpose of being married in another state without having first acquired a domicile in said State, and shall return to the State of Louisiana to reside permanently, after having contracted marriage in another State."[58] This clearly reached the evasion case, but equally clearly it excluded the migratory case.

The 1879 Texas Penal Code provided that "[i]f any white person and negro shall knowingly intermarry with each other within this state, *or having so intermarried, in or out of the state,*

shall continue to live together as man and wife within this state,
they shall be punished by confinement in the penitentiary for
a term not less than two nor more than five years."[59] This provision might be construed to mean that cohabitation within
Texas was punishable even if the couple had married outside
the state. On the other hand, the words "continue to" suggest
that this law applied only to evasion cases and did not apply
to couples who already were married when they first moved to
the state. Such a couple could not "continue" a practice—living
together as man and wife in Texas—that they had never en-
gaged in previously. The second interpretation seems to be the
sounder one, but it is impossible to be sure because no case
interpreting the provision appears in the reports.[60]

As for the case law, it was divided. We already examined
the *Ross* case, where a migratory marriage was recognized. The
same result was reached in *Bonds v. Foster.*[61] A. H. Foster, who
owned a slave named Leah in Louisiana, moved to Ohio, freed
her and the children she had borne by him, and set up a home
for them there. Under Ohio law, that was apparently sufficient
to create a common law marriage. After a few years he moved
the family to Texas, where he died in 1867. His executor sold his
home to pay his debts, and Leah sued the executor, claiming
that as Foster's wife her property was exempt from sale for the
payment of debts. Texas at the time had a law against interracial
marriage.[62] Despite that law, the court ruled in Leah's favor. It
held that if they were married in Ohio, then their moving to
Texas "did not, *per se,* operate a dissolution of the marriage,
although, at the time, none of the marital rights of the parties
could have been enforced by the laws of Texas."[63]

A 1928 case from California is peculiar and hard to clas-
sify. It involved the legitimacy, and so eligibility to inherit, of
Susan O. Casey, born in New Orleans in 1864. Her father was

white, her mother mulatto. She sought to inherit the estate of Annie Morgan, who she claimed was her half-sister, with the same father but a different mother (who was also mulatto). Annie was born in Mississippi in 1858; her mother died when she was about three years old. There was no evidence that either woman's parents had ever gone through a marriage ceremony, but, Susan argued, there was a legal presumption, codified in California law, that a man and woman who live together for years as if they were husband and wife are lawfully married. If the marriages were found to exist, that would bolster Susan's claim that Annie was her half-sister. The Supreme Court of California refused to apply the presumption. "It has been the law of this state from its earliest days, and long before either Annie Morgan or Susan O. Casey was born, that a marriage between a white person and a mulatto was illegal," the court declared. "In the absence of any evidence to the contrary we must presume that the laws of the state of Mississippi and Louisiana are and were the same. With an express statutory inhibition against a marriage between persons of these two races, no presumption can be indulged in that this law was violated and a marriage entered into between these parties."[64] As it happened, the court's presumption was correct. Louisiana had a statute banning interracial marriage in 1864.[65] Mississippi in 1858 reached the same result by a more circuitous route: the right to marry was limited to free whites. This case's crude presumption, which is of interest mainly as evidence of the inadequacy of the California Supreme Court's law library in 1928, might be taken to imply hostility to migratory marriages. However, the court said nothing about what it would do if the presumption were rebutted by evidence that the foreign law was in fact different—that the marriage was valid under that law.

There have been two cases in which the *Ross* dissenters'
position prevailed, but neither of these adopted a blanket rule
of nonrecognition (and only one of them concerned interracial
marriage). In *State v. Bell*,[66] a white man and a black woman
married in Mississippi, where they then resided,[67] and later
moved to Tennessee, where the husband was arrested and
tried. He pleaded the Mississippi marriage as a defense. The
Tennessee Supreme Court rejected the defense, thundering
that if it were accepted "we might have in Tennessee the father
living with his daughter, the son with the mother, the brother
with the sister, in lawful wedlock, because they had formed
such relations in a state or country where they were not prohibited. The Turk or Mohammedan, with his numerous wives,
may establish his harem at the doors of the capitol, and we are
without remedy. Yet none of these are more revolting, more to
be avoided, or more unnatural than the case before us."[68]

Even *Bell*, however, does not necessarily entail a blanket
rule of nonrecognition. Years later, U.S. Supreme Court Justice
Harlan Fiske Stone interpreted the case narrowly, as holding
that "[w]ithout denying the validity of a marriage in another
state, the privileges flowing from marriage may be subject to
the local law."[69] Similarly, Herbert Goodrich, writing in 1927,
would concede only that "[c]ertain incidents of the marriage
relationship may be refused recognition if they involve a violation of public policy or good morals of the law of the forum."[70]
On this account, the couple in *Bell* remained married; they
simply were not permitted the incident of cohabitation in certain states.

A similar interpretation can be offered for *State v. Brown*,[71]
an 1890 Ohio case in which an uncle was prosecuted for intercourse with his niece, whom he had married in another state
where they then lived. The court held that "we are not bound,

upon principles of comity, to permit persons to violate our criminal laws, adopted in the interest of decency and good morals, and based on principles of sound public policy, because they have assumed, in another state or country where it was lawful, the relation which led to the acts prohibited by our laws."[72] The last part of the quoted sentence appears to concede that the couple *has* assumed the relation of man and wife; presumably, neither would have been permitted to come to Ohio alone and there marry someone else. Nonetheless, their kinship status meant that they could not lawfully engage in sexual intercourse within the borders of Ohio.

Visitors and Already Existing Marriages

A few other miscegenation cases are pertinent, even though they do not squarely reach the question presented in *Ross* and *Bell*.[73] A federal district court attempted to adjudicate between these competing visions of comity in *Ex parte Kinney*,[74] the evasion case we considered earlier, in which an evasive marriage in Washington, D.C., was denied recognition in Virginia. *Kinney* is the only miscegenation case that contains any discussion of constitutional limitations deriving from federalism (rather than from the equal protection clause of the Fourteenth Amendment).

The federal court in *Kinney* took a hard line on the question that had lately divided the high courts of North Carolina and Tennessee in *Ross* and *Bell*, declaring that Edmund Kinney's claim would be rejected even in a closer case, involving "citizens of another state, lawfully married in that domicile, afterward migrating thence in good faith into this state."[75]

But the court also declared that Virginia could not enforce its law against nondomiciliaries, nor exclude altogether interracial couples domiciled in the District of Columbia: "That such a citizen would have a right of transit with his wife through Virginia, and of temporary stoppage, and of carrying on any business here not requiring residence, may be conceded, because these are privileges following a citizen of the United States."[76] The reference to "temporary stoppage" clearly implies that Virginia might have to tolerate within its borders sexual intercourse between a black man and a white woman.

There were also a few cases in which the interracial couple had married in the forum state before the statutory prohibition of miscegenation was adopted. (The same problem will arise if Massachusetts, where thousands of same-sex marriages have been celebrated, votes to ban such marriages.) In these cases, the marriage was invariably recognized.[77] The most fully reasoned of these cases deemed it dispositive that the parties in the case before the court were entitled to marry when they did: "They did not then bring into this state an institution disfavored by a declared policy. They remained where they were domiciled, as many others did, and had a right to do. The law of their domicile was changed."[78] Thus, the policy of preserving existing marriages overrode the policy against intermarriage: "[A]n act designed to wipe out, by the wholesale, legal, existing marriages between members of the white and black races would be almost profligate in its tendency."[79]

The courts reached these results even though the miscegenation statutes were very strongly worded, usually declaring interracial marriages "void."[80] The cases described earlier, which held that the miscegenation laws did not reach extraterritorial marriages not involving cohabitation in the state, all involved statutes using this term. In general, when presented with language of this kind, courts have been reluctant to apply the restriction to domiciliaries of other states.[81]

All this, of course, has implications for same-sex marriage. These precedents hold that even an exceedingly strong public policy does not entail a blanket rule of nonrecognition. Finer distinctions have to be drawn.

As these miscegenation cases arose out of a despicable regime, it can seem odd, at best, to invoke them as authority for anything in contemporary law. The very idea of legality was caricatured when judges reasoned out the consequences of that regime in this bland, workmanlike way. But the southern judges did have something intelligent to say about how to deal with deep moral disagreement. The question for us today is whether we can manage at least the minimal level of decency and mutual respect that existed in the awful years of legalized racism.

These cases left some important problems unsolved. They were split about the status of migratory marriages, though they tended to recognize them. And we have only one passing dictum, from *Kinney*, on the important question of visitor marriages, when a member of a forbidden marriage is simply passing through the state. These questions did not arise in the Jim Crow courts because the regime of the postbellum South was not fully a regime of law at all. The most important sanctions were enforced, not by law, but by private violence, with the state's active or passive approval. Interracial couples attempting to travel through the deep South would not have been tried for miscegenation. They would have been lynched, and the local police would have ignored or even participated in the violence.

There is also not a single case in which someone tried to use the differences in states' laws in order to evade financial obligations, to one's spouse or one's children or one's creditors. This is probably because, during this time, it was so easy to

leave a marriage by informal means. In a large country without national recordkeeping, it was a simple matter to leave town
with no forwarding address and start life in a new place where
one's past was unknown.[82] Under these circumstances, there
was neither the need nor the opportunity for formal litigation
about the status of one's marriage.

This chapter has focused on appellate cases and statutes,
but official recognition can be accompanied by more or less
hostility in practice. In Oklahoma in 1961, Vernon Thomas and
his wife Bettye narrowly escaped prosecution for having married in Kansas. (It is impossible to tell from the scanty news
reports where they lived at the time of the marriage.) First,
Vernon was arrested for driving without a permit, even though
he was not driving when he was arrested. Then Bettye was
arrested for speeding, at a time when her car was parked. Then
authorities searched their home on the pretext that a neighbor
had complained about a loud party. Finally, three weeks after
that, the authorities got to the point by arresting the couple for
miscegenation. The charge was dismissed on the grounds
that Oklahoma courts had no jurisdiction over a Kansas ceremony.[83] The Oklahoma authorities had no official basis for
treating the couple badly, but that did not prevent persistent,
low-level harassment.

Even the strongest arguments against same-sex marriage
made today disavow that level of hostility. In every state in the
United States, visiting same-sex couples are entitled to the protection of the law. And this means that the courts must reckon
with the question of their legal status.

IV

The Stakes

We have looked at many stories and will look at more. But ultimately, the question of interstate marriage recognition is not just a question about particular individuals. Gay people, it has sometimes been remarked, have all the "good" stories on their side: partners heartlessly kept away from hospital deathbeds, families deprived of health insurance and pensions. But they have still lost the fight over same-sex marriage in most states because most Americans are convinced that these stories are outweighed by principles that dictate that marriage can only be between a man and a woman. The same-sex marriage controversy is a struggle between visions of the good life. We must now consider these differing visions and how they each can be given a place in the American polity.

We noted in Chapter 2 that courts today generally address choice of law problems by using what is called *interest analysis:* they try to discern the legitimate interest each state has in applying its own law, and then they try to decide the dispute before them in a way that accommodates all of those interests to the greatest extent feasible. In choice of law cases involving same-sex marriage, if the forum has an interest, declared in a state law, in denying recognition to such marriage, a court must still determine what this interest is and the limits of its legitimate application. This chapter will try to describe this interest with precision.

The same-sex marriage debate raises three questions, which stand in complex relations to one another. First, which relationships ought to receive symbolic approval from the state? Second, which relationships should have tangible legal consequences, such as the right to inherit property or to make medical decisions for another person? And third, how ought the state to cope with outright prejudice against gays, which remains a potent force in American culture and which most articulate opponents of same-sex marriage repudiate?

In many ways, the present controversy is analogous to the old miscegenation question. But there are important differences. The miscegenation decisions rarely gave much weight to the right of citizens to travel or to the interests of states that *recognized* interracial marriages in giving effect to their own laws. I have not been able to find a single case in which a member of an interracial couple sought to evade financial obligations by crossing state lines. The southern states aimed at maintaining the status quo of white supremacy, which interracial marriage would have threatened. They wanted above all to prevent interracial couples from living as married within their borders. (They had a much more indulgent attitude toward white men keeping black concubines because such relationships did not question the racial hierarchy.)

Today, however, no state can, or avowedly intends to, keep all gay people out. Any interest in preventing homosexual sex from taking place is now illegitimate after *Lawrence v. Texas,*[1] in which the Supreme Court declared that laws banning homosexual sex are unconstitutional.[2]

The interests of a state such as Massachusetts, which recognizes same-sex marriages, are clear. Massachusetts regulates its own citizens' relationships, conferring rights and obligations, and it wants those rights and obligations to remain enforceable even when the parties travel out of state. But what is the countervailing interest of the states that have a strong public policy against same-sex marriage? To answer this question, it is necessary first to step back and construct a conceptual map of the controversy over same-sex marriage. This controversy involves a confusing collection of issues. Questions about health insurance and hospital visitation intersect with deeper ones about which family forms are valued and who is a full citizen. And at the center of it all is the emotionally fraught word "marriage." In order to clarify the state interests at stake, I will begin by disentangling what the underlying debate is really about.

The Two Debates about Same-Sex Marriage

One reason why the debate is so muddled is that we are really having two debates at once: a normative debate and an administrative debate. The first is about what relationships to value or even to sanctify. The second is about administration—about which relationships ought to have legal consequences.

The *normative debate* concerns what relationships are intrinsically good or bad. This discussion is not just a legal one. It is taking place within most religious denominations within the United States, creating divisions that sometimes approach schism.[3] Opposition to same-sex marriage as a normative matter relies on two distinct (though not incompatible) claims. One pertains to the intrinsic essence of marriage. The other concerns the possible consequences of recognizing same-sex marriage.

According to the intrinsic-essence view, sex can be morally worthy precisely and only because of its relation to procreation. Even the marriages of infertile heterosexual couples take their meaning from the fact that they form a union of the pro-creative kind, and their bodily union therefore has procreative significance. Whatever other value same-sex couples may achieve, marriage is impossible for them because it is inherently heterosexual. From this perspective, the movement for same-sex marriage is a misguided attempt to deny fundamental moral distinctions about the nature of marriage.[4]

The consequentialist argument against same-sex marriage avoids such controversial value claims. Instead, it maintains that indisputably bad consequences will follow if same-sex marriage is recognized. Thus Maggie Gallagher argues that same-sex marriage "affirms that children do not need mothers and fathers, and that marriage has nothing to do with babies."[5] Recognition of such marriages, she writes, will send a destructive message to society: that marriage is "an essentially private, intimate, emotional relationship created by two people for their own personal reasons to enhance their own personal well-being."[6] If the state endorses this message, there will be an increase in "poverty and trauma caused by widespread fatherlessness."[7]

Opposition to same-sex marriage may or may not be linked to the view that homosexual relations are intrinsically wrong. Many Americans detach the two issues. The number of Americans who oppose same-sex marriage considerably-exceeds the number who think that homosexual conduct is always wrong.[8]

Supporters of same-sex marriage accept none of this, of course. They think that sex is valuable, either in itself or because it draws us toward friendship of a singular degree and kind. This bringing together of people is worthwhile, whether or not it leads to childbearing or child rearing. On this account, sexuality is linked to the flourishing of the next generation only to the extent that it is one of a number of factors that can bond adults together into stable familial units in which children are likely to thrive. It is not necessary or even important that the children be the biological product of the adults' sex acts. What makes a family a good one is the adults' care for one another and the creation of a family environment in which children can thrive. Many gay people have stable, loving households and are raising children very competently.[9] From this perspective, it is the devaluation of same-sex intimacy that is immoral because it reflects arbitrary and irrational discrimination.

This is the normative debate. Proponents claim that same-sex relationships can be just as valuable as heterosexual marriages. Opponents say either that same-sex relationships are intrinsically inferior to heterosexual relationships or that recognizing same-sex marriage will send a bad message, with damaging effects on heterosexual families.

The *administrative debate* concerns the way society should allocate its resources and protect its citizens' interests. Like it or not, households, of whatever kind exist. So do relationships of dependency within those households. It can reasonably be inferred what members of those households would want and need if some unprovided-for contingency arises, such as illness or death. From this perspective, law ought to maximize people's welfare, either by reflecting people's preferences and providing the default options that they would probably have chosen had they been able to think about it, or by providing them with services that everyone needs. Adequate health care is one example.

The task of constructing the law of marriage is, from an administrative perspective, analogous to the task of constructing the law of business corporations:[10] How can the state maximize efficiency and satisfy people's preferences about their relationships by constructing sensible "one size fits all" default rules, while protecting the interests of third parties, notably children? Here it all turns on what we know about the effects of various practices and policies. And issues of sanctification are very far from our minds.

Separating Normative from Administrative Questions

A central difficulty in the same-sex marriage debate is that in it administrative issues are held hostage to normative ones. Any administrative accommodation is seen as a fatal concession of symbolic ground. This is unfortunate, because one can address the administrative question of how to tend to citizens' needs without taking any position on the moral one.

There have been attempts to separate the two. The most common, followed in many jurisdictions, is to grant same-sex couples some or all of the rights of married couples without the honorific of "marriage," under the rubric of "domestic partnerships" or "civil unions." This has happened in Vermont, California, and Connecticut and also outside the United States. Denmark, Sweden, Norway, Finland, Iceland, and the United Kingdom have partnerships that are nearly identical to marriage, while a more limited set of rights and responsibilities is available to same-sex couples in France, Germany, Belgium,

Austria, Hungary, Portugal, Brazil, Croatia, the Czech Republic, New Zealand, and parts of Australia, Argentina, Switzerland, and South Africa (which, under orders from its Supreme
Court, is about to switch to full marriage recognition).[11] The
U.S. constitutional amendment failed in part because it was so
broadly worded that it seemed to some to prohibit civil unions
as well as same-sex marriages.

The civil union strategy is in many ways an attractive
compromise. Americans oppose same-sex marriage by over-
whelming margins. But polls also show that the label of "marriage" is all that many people really care about. As long as that
line isn't crossed, they are quite willing to let the law recognize
same-sex relationships.[12] In Vermont, Connecticut, and California, civil unions and domestic partnerships give same-sex
couples nearly all the legal benefits of marriage.[13] When California enacted its law, with no prodding from any court, the
legislation was so uncontroversial that the national press hardly
even picked up the story.[14]

But not everyone can live with this solution. Many gay
couples want the law to give its imprimatur to their relationships in the same way it does for heterosexual couples. Moreover, gay people don't want second-class status, and that's what
civil unions amount to.[15] They are unwilling to concede that
their relationships are in any way inferior to heterosexual
marriages: couples of both types are equally able to form
households, care for each other, and create environments in
which children can thrive.[16] The Massachusetts Supreme Judicial Court held that the civil union compromise was constitutionally inadequate because the court "would have the
effect of maintaining and fostering a stigma of exclusion that
the Constitution prohibits."[17] "Separate but equal" has an un-
attractive history.

Conservatives have also objected to the civil union compromise on symbolic grounds: such unions give state recognition to homosexual relationships as such, and that, they think, would be wrong. (For this reason, some states have enacted laws barring recognition of civil unions as well as same-sex marriages; see Chapter 9.) But these same conservatives do not object to the use of neutral legal instruments to accommodate such relationships. They typically argue that many of the legal effects of marriage can be accomplished by wills, contracts, powers of attorney, and other generally available legal instruments. (Thus, for example, President George W. Bush has suggested that gay couples can secure many of the benefits of marriage, such as the right to hospital visitation, through civil contracts.[18]) In making this argument, they implicitly reject the result in the *Kaufmann* case, described in Chapter 1, which held, in effect, that such instruments would not be given effect if gay people used them. In short, they offer their own way of separating the administrative from the symbolic.

The Power and Limits
of the Racism Analogy

A state's ability to symbolically reject same-sex marriage is limited by a second symbolic concern, one that the state is constitutionally required to consider. This is the state's obligation not to give its imprimatur to bigotry. No state can have a legitimate interest in declaring that gay people are inferior, degraded human beings.

This last limitation arises from the Fourteenth Amendment's requirement of "equal protection of the laws." This requirement, the Supreme Court has repeatedly said, means that states are forbidden to brand any class of citizens as intrinsically inferior. Thus in *Strauder v. West Virginia,* the first race discrimination case to reach the Supreme Court after the Civil War, the Court struck down a state law excluding blacks from juries. The Court declared that the Fourteenth Amendment protects blacks "from legal discriminations, implying inferiority in civil society."[19] The *Strauder* Court held that the exclusion was "practically a brand upon them, affixed by the law, an assertion of their inferiority, and a stimulant to that race prejudice which is an impediment to securing to individuals of the race that equal justice which the law aims to secure to all others."[20] *Plessy v. Ferguson,* the infamous 1896 case that upheld racial segregation, offered the tribute that vice pays to virtue when it declared that a segregation law *would* be unconstitutional if it were true that it "stamps the colored race with a badge of inferiority."[21] *Brown v. Board of Education* held that the segregation of black students is impermissible because it "generates a feeling of inferiority as to their status in the community that may affect their hearts and minds in a way unlikely ever to be undone."[22]

Is discrimination against gay people the moral and constitutional equivalent of racism? If it is, then the state's symbolic interest in nonrecognition is entitled to no weight at all, no more than in the case of interracial marriage. This is what is often claimed by those who press the analogy with the miscegenation cases.[23] The Supreme Court ultimately concluded that the laws against interracial marriage served an entirely illegitimate purpose: maintaining white supremacy. Once it decided that, those laws were dead.

There is some truth in the racism analogy. But it is not obviously the whole truth, and so the analogy does not delegitimize all state interests in refusing recognition to same-sex marriages.

Ample evidence shows that American culture is contaminated by prejudice against gays that is morally and constitutionally equivalent to racism. This kind of bigotry is a familiar part of the culture, with its most obvious manifestation in the gangs, present in every major city in the country, that violently attack strangers whom they believe to be gay. Attacks on gays, often involving torture and mutilation, bespeak an astonishing rage. Such attacks are common and constantly occur throughout the United States.[24] And it is not only marginal thugs who mistreat gay people; a recent survey by Amnesty International found that gays are frequently abused by the police as well.[25]

The stigma against gay people is most profound among adolescents. A study of harassment in American high schools found that the most upsetting type of harassment was to be called gay.[26] One national survey of males aged fifteen to nineteen found that 89 percent thought that the idea of homosexual sexual activity was "disgusting," and only 12 percent were sure that they could befriend an openly gay male.[27] Students are often conspicuously cruel to their peers whom they perceive as gay, often publicly humiliating them, threatening harm, and spitting at, pushing, or physically attacking them. Adults in authority often do nothing about the harassment, and sometimes they blame the victims.[28] Hatred of gays thus appears to be an element of the normal socialization of American youth.

Gordon Allport's classic study of prejudice notes that when hate-motivated violence occurs, its perpetrators tend to be acting on attitudes that are held in milder form throughout the culture in which they have been socialized.[29] Although few Americans actually engage in violence against gays, many more dislike them intensely.

Attitudes toward gay people until very recently were over-whelmingly negative. As recently as 1994, gays were among the least liked groups in the United States, according to Kenneth Sherrill's analysis of the Feeling Thermometers of the American National Election Study. Respondents were asked to rate their feelings toward a variety of groups on a scale of zero to one hundred. In four surveys spanning a ten-year period, the lowest score, zero, was consistently assigned to gays and lesbians by more respondents than any other group; next in order were illegal immigrants, people on welfare, and Christian fundamentalists. (In 1994, the most recent year in Sherrill's analysis, 28.2 percent assigned gays a zero ranking, as compared with 24.2 percent for the next most unpopular group, illegal immigrants, and 9.1 percent for the third most unpopular group, people on welfare. The figure for blacks was 2.0 percent.) Sherrill concluded that "such hostility does not face any other group in the electorate."[30] The hostility was not only intense, but widespread. Gays and lesbians consistently had received one of the lowest mean FT scores, though in recent years they had escaped the lowest average rating by being two to four points above illegal immigrants. "Among American citizens included in these studies," Sherrill writes, "only lesbians and gay men were the objects of cold feelings from a majority of Americans."[31]

More recent data show some improvement. Morris Fiorina's review in 2005 found that the proportion of Americans giving gay people a zero rating "has steadily declined, from almost a third in 1988 to less than 10 percent in 2000. Along with this sharp decline in extreme dislike, the average ratings of gays and lesbians have climbed significantly in the past fifteen years."[32] But these recent data should not be overread. Negative feelings that are as deeply rooted as this one do not just disappear, even if they are consciously repudiated. Compare the case of race. Almost no one is willing to admit to racism today, yet it continues to unconsciously affect decision making in countless ways, from employment decisions to political advertisements.[33]

The idea that gays are inferior human beings is not the only reason they are discriminated against, but it is plainly one of the reasons. Perhaps the most direct window into American culture is its ordinary language. Richard Mohr notes that the English language does not treat gay people merely as people who engage in certain sexual activities:

> With the apparent exception of "cocksucker," no widespread antigay slur gives any indication that its censure is directed at sex acts rather than despised social status. Group-directed slurs (dyke, queer, fag) place gays in a significant social category along with blacks (nigger, shine, shitskin), other racial groups (chink), women (cunt, gash), various ethnic groups (wop, dago, gook, jap, JAP, mick, kike). . . . It does not place gays in the same category as liars, hypocrites, murderers, and thieves—those who commit immoral and criminal actions and yet for whom culture in no case has coined group-based invectives. This schema of slurs strongly suggests that gay men and lesbians are held to be immoral because they are hated, rather than hated because they are immoral.[34]

Even homosexuals who do not act on, or even who openly repudiate, their inclinations still bear the stigma of their status, if it is known. In 1976, presidential candidate Jimmy Carter told an interviewer, "I've looked on a lot of women with lust. I've committed adultery in my heart many times. This is something God recognizes I will do—and I have done it—and God forgives me for it."[35] The statement caused a minor flap at the time, but Carter went on to win the election. Imagine the reaction then, or even today, if he had said that he had looked on a lot of men with lust.

All this is, however, only part of the story.

As noted earlier, many people hold the traditional view that homosexual acts are per se worthless and harmful. Others think that marriage is intrinsically heterosexual. Still others resist same-sex marriage because they want marriage to maintain its symbolic link with procreation and think that, by severing that link, same-sex marriage would damage heterosexual families. They all want to prevent their states from endorsing moral propositions that they regard as false or damaging or both. You may disagree with these views, but none of them necessarily denies the human dignity and worth of gay people. To see the limits of the racism analogy, it may be helpful to examine with some care just what is morally objectionable about racism.

Anthony Appiah distinguishes between two different kinds of racist ideas. One, which he calls *extrinsic racism,* claims that race entails morally relevant qualities, such as honesty or courage (or the lack thereof), which are uncontroversially proper bases for treating people differently. *Intrinsic racism,* on the other hand, holds "that each race has a different moral status, quite independent of the moral characteristics entailed by its racial essence."[36]

Intrinsic racism, unlike extrinsic racism, is not rebuttable by evidence. It holds some people inferior regardless of what they think or do. Intrinsic racism is *essentially malign:* it directly contradicts one of the foundational ideas of human rights—that all human beings have intrinsic dignity and worth. One can morally condemn intrinsic racism without needing to undertake any further investigation. Intrinsic racism is evil in any world that we can imagine.

Extrinsic racism may be just as evil as intrinsic racism, but the path to that conclusion is less direct. This is because extrinsic racism relies on claims that *would* be relevant if they were true. It either is or is not the case that black people are stupid, lazy, and prone to criminality. It is now well established that these familiar racist stereotypes are false, but this took some work, and it was important to do that work. Such claims are *contingently malign:* they are malign only if certain claims, not necessarily connected to foundational issues of human worth, turn out to be correct.

A similar distinction can be drawn among antigay attitudes. Some of these attitudes are essentially malign: they condemn gay people as intrinsically inferior. These are what we have been examining: common slurs that brand gays as intrinsically defective, violent acting out that strikes at their very existence. But the objections to same-sex marriage that we have been considering are not of that kind. They assert claims about the nature of marriage that are logically independent of any claim about the moral worth of gay people.

Such claims might still turn out to be malign. Extrinsic racism is still racism. It might be the case that the racism analogy is entirely valid. Perhaps conservative objections to gay rights are unfounded and so pointlessly inflict real harm on gay people. But this conclusion is dependent on some substantive moral argument that engages with the conservative views. The racism analogy cannot do that. It is a conclusion, not an argument.

Most importantly for our purposes, deciding whether the racism analogy is appropriate here would require us to engage the core moral question of whether homosexual sex really is no worse than heterosexual sex. The analogy does not take us around that question; it steers us straight into it.

To complicate matters, here, unlike in the racism case, the contingencies in dispute are normative rather than empirical. It was not very hard to show that racist stereotypes rested on terrible science. Questions of ultimate value, on the other hand, are notoriously resistant to rational resolution. Decent people conscientiously come to different views about whether same-sex relationships can be morally equivalent to opposite-sex relationships. They also reasonably disagree about the likely consequences of innovative social reforms.

Many traditionalists have even recognized the existence of antigay prejudice of the intrinsically malign kind and have repudiated it. The Catholic Church, for example, has condemned antigay bigotry and violence while maintaining its condemnation of homosexual activity.[37] The Church's doctrine does not entail that a person is morally defective and unclean merely because of homosexual desire. Quite the contrary: "the particular inclination of the homosexual person is not a sin."[38] The equal dignity of all human beings is a foundational belief in Christianity; as a historical matter, Christianity is where contemporary secular liberals got the idea.

The upshot is that both antigay prejudice, of an essentially malign kind, and serious moral objections, which are not essentially malign, are likely to be at work behind any law that expressly disadvantages gay people—such as a ban on same-sex marriage. And this means that one cannot rule out the possibility that a state that wants to ban same-sex marriage is doing so for legitimate reasons.

How can one decide which purpose predominates in any law? A key consideration, I would suggest, is whether the law expresses a moral view while taking some regard for the fact that gay people exist, have a right to exist, and have legitimate concerns of their own, or whether on the other hand it indiscriminately lashes out at them.

Essentially malign prejudice does not consist only of a desire to harm the disfavored group. Paul Brest notes that racism can take the form of "racially selective sympathy and indifference," meaning "the unconscious failure to extend to a minority the same recognition of humanity, and hence the same sympathy and care, given as a matter of course to one's own group."[39] A classic example comes from Mark Twain's account of a conversation between Huckleberry Finn and Aunt Sally:

> "We blowed out a cylinder-head."
> "Good gracious! anybody hurt?"
> "No'm. Killed a nigger."
> "Well, it's lucky; because sometimes people do get
>   hurt."[40]

Where prejudice is pervasive, there are grounds for suspicion that selective sympathy and indifference are at work. That suspicion will ripen into proof, not only if a disfavored group is targeted for harm, but also if no weight is being given to the disfavored group's interests.

This limits the degree to which a state can legitimately invoke its symbolic interest in avoiding endorsement of same-sex marriage. There is a danger in invoking symbolic concerns. Symbolism can rationalize anything. For many years, the criminalization of homosexual sex in the United States was justified on this basis: if the law stopped hunting down gays' private sex acts, it was argued, this would implicitly send a message of approval.[41] M. J. Sydenham's history of the French Revolution explains the execution of Danton and his followers as resting on similar symbolic considerations: "If they were left alive after their opponents had been killed their position would be relatively stronger, and it would appear that the Committee [of Public Safety] had acted at their command."[42] Symbolic politics can generate extraordinarily brutal policies.

Steven D. Smith observes that perceptions of symbolic endorsement are parasitic on one's background norms of appropriate, neutral behavior. Thus, for example, the First Amendment's establishment clause prohibits the state from supporting religion, but no one thinks that it is violated when a church is burning and the fire department puts it out. This is not endorsement. It is just what fire departments do. On the other hand, the state would certainly be sending a symbolic message if the firefighters stood by and watched the church burn.[43] More generally, the cultural meaning of behavior depends on background cultural norms, which change over time. Baseball teams aren't now understood to be making a statement when they add well-qualified players to their rosters—that's just what baseball teams do—but the Brooklyn Dodgers necessarily and inevitably made a statement when they decided to hire Jackie Robinson in 1947.

The question of whether a state has symbolically "endorsed" homosexual marriage, then, depends on one's background assumptions about what sort of action is normally appropriate. If one is behaving appropriately, then one is behaving neutrally and avoiding improper favoritism.[44] The idea of "endorsement" is always parasitic in this way. Following the unspoken norm endorses nothing. Only departing from the norm sends a message.

What is the implicit norm behind the idea that states endorse same-sex marriage if they treat same-sex couples as people with legitimate family interests and obligations, just like anyone else? It would have to be one of ostracizing gays, of pretending that they do not exist, and of giving no weight to their interests. If a state's symbolic interest is construed so broadly, then the result coincides too conveniently with what it would be if it unapologetically reflected hatred toward gay people.

States with strong public policies against same-sex marriage should understand themselves to have two different symbolic aims. The first is to set forth clearly their own view that marriage is inherently heterosexual. The second is to make clear that this view is not based on prejudice. The best way to combine these aims is to adopt rules that do not entirely ignore gay couples' administrative interests.

The upshot of this analysis is that, if a law implements objections to same-sex marriage in a way that gives no weight to the legitimate interests of gay couples, or that even reaches out to harm those interests, then it has crossed the line into endorsement of bigotry. A state has no legitimate interest in expressing its hatred of gay people or its desire for their nonexistence. If, on the other hand, it expresses that public policy in a more measured way, then its public policy is entitled to some weight in a court's choice of law analysis. To say it again, the symbolic and administrative concerns raised by same-sex marriage are separable. There are plenty of ways to administratively accommodate same-sex relationships from other states without calling them marriages. The rest of this book will consider how this might be done.

V

Against Blanket Nonrecognition

In 1852, Jonathan Lemmon and his wife left Virginia for Texas. Evidently economic hardship was part of the reason. They were poor. Nearly all the property they had in the world was eight slaves.

Naturally, they brought the slaves along. Traveling overland was expensive and slow in those days, and the easiest way to go was by boat. But there was no direct steamship service between any port in Maryland and the Gulf Coast. The usual route was to go first to New York, then change boats and take a steamboat to New Orleans.

Ignoring warnings not to take their slaves ashore, they went to a hotel, where they planned to wait the three days for the New Orleans boat. There they were discovered by a free black, who hurried to court and petitioned for a writ of habeas corpus. The trial court freed the slaves. Jonathan Lemmon took his case to the New York Court of Appeals, the highest court in the state, but there he lost again.[1]

The court of appeals held that a slave from Virginia became free the instant he or she set foot on New York soil because slavery could not exist in New York. New York statutory law so held, and that law was constitutional: "Every sovereign State has a right to determine by its laws the condition of all persons who may at any time be within its jurisdiction; to exclude therefrom those whose introduction would contravene its policy, or to declare the conditions upon which they may be received."[2] The Constitution contained an exception for fugitive slaves, who had to be returned to their owners, but that was the only exception to the general rule.[3] The state's interest in being free of slavery did not become less when the slave was merely transient. As the court put it in a concurring opinion, "[I]t is the *status,* the unjust and unnatural relation, which the policy of the State aims to suppress, and her policy fails, at least in part, if the *status* be upheld at all."[4]

A state might want to say that same-sex marriages are so abominable that they will not be recognized, ever, for any purposes. Just as slavery could not exist in New York, one might argue, a state can legitimately decide that same-sex marriage simply cannot exist within its borders. One might say, as the *Ross* dissenters said of interracial marriage, that the relation is "severed the instant they set foot upon our soil" and that "individuals who have formed relations which are obnoxious to our laws can find their comfort in staying away from us."[5] By this logic, any obligations created by a same-sex marriage would evaporate the instant the affected party set foot within the borders of such a state.[6]

This kind of blanket rule of nonrecognition, analogous to that proposed in *Lemmon v. People,* is unworkable and has four fatal difficulties. First, a blanket nonrecognition rule produces absurd and cruel results. Second, the rule is inconsistent with the rights of citizens within the federal system. Third, it would violate rights to equal protection established by the

Fourteenth Amendment because it would reflect a bare desire to harm a politically unpopular group. And fourth, it cannot be justified even in terms of the strongest and most attractive version of the conservative case against same-sex marriage.

Absurd Results

The consequences of the blanket nonrecognition rule, which we have been exploring throughout the book, can briefly be summarized:

- Parties to marriages could dissolve the marriages without any obligation to account for the marital assets, possibly leaving a dependent spouse deprived of assets that that spouse has spent years helping to amass.
- More generally, blanket nonrecognition would mean that states following this rule would become havens for people wanting to avoid obligations of spousal property and child support that they had validly entered into.

Joseph Singer has offered a plausible scenario that illustrates these last two points.[7] Suppose that Anne and Lily marry in Massachusetts and then, ten years later, move to Seattle because Lily's mother, Miriam, who lives there, is ill. They move into Miriam's house. Anne sells the Massachusetts house and invests the money in bonds. Three years later they separate, and Lily sues Anne for divorce in state court in Washington.

Washington statutes provide that marriages between two people of the same sex are "prohibited" and that a marriage that is prohibited in Washington will not be recognized as "valid" in Washington even if it is "recognized as valid in another jurisdiction."[8] Washington law allows plaintiffs to divorce if they live in Washington and are married, and a court may equitably divide their property. But under Washington law, Anne and Lily are not married.

Lily thus can get a divorce only by relocating to Massachusetts and establishing a domicile there. But even if she does that, the Massachusetts court will not have jurisdiction to award alimony or an equitable division of property because Anne does not live in Massachusetts. To accomplish that, Lily must return to Washington and get the Washington courts to recognize the divorce and then distribute the property. (Under the doctrine of "divisible divorce," Massachusetts could have the power to grant Lily a divorce but no power over Anne's property or personal obligations; Lily has to go to a state that has the right to assert its power over Anne in order to make claims upon her.) But under blanket nonrecognition, Washington courts will not recognize the marriage or the subsequent divorce. Lily would be entirely without a remedy. Anne would get to keep all the assets that they have accumulated together over thirteen years of married life.

- Travelers to a state that would not recognize marital rights and obligations would not be able to rely on those rights and obligations should the need unexpectedly arise.

Suppose Jane, who is married in Massachusetts to Sally, travels on business to Virginia and there is hurt in a car crash and hospitalized. Sally would not be permitted to make medical decisions for Jane in Virginia. She might not even be permitted to visit her in the hospital. And if Jane is unable to make her own decisions, Sally would have no authority to take her back to Massachusetts.

- If the children of same-sex relationships were brought into a state with a blanket nonrecognition rule, voluntarily or by force, their non-biological parents would have no right to get them back.

If Jane were the biological mother of Adam, and Adam were injured in the same crash, Sally could not make medical decisions for him, or visit him, either. Under the blanket non-recognition rule, this is what she would be told: "You may not visit Jane or Adam because only family members may visit patients here, and you are not a family member of either of these people in any respect that our state recognizes. You may not participate in medical decisions for either of them. If Jane dies, you will not have any parental rights with regard to Adam. When he recovers, the hospital cannot release him to you, and you cannot take him back to Massachusetts with you. If there is no surviving biological relative, we will regard Adam as an orphan and place him in foster care."

The same thing would happen if, after Jane had died, Adam was kidnapped from his backyard by a stranger and carried across state lines. The kidnapper doubtless would be prosecuted, but Adam would still end up in foster care.

- A blanket nonrecognition rule would also be convenient for nonbiological parents who want to be free from child support obligations if the couple separates.

In our first scenario, if Lily had borne a child during the marriage with Anne's support and encouragement, then Anne would probably have obligations of support.[9] Yet Anne could avoid all obligations to the child by moving to Washington.

- A same-sex spouse could marry again in another state without having to dissolve the earlier marriage or even having to disclose to the new spouse the existence of the previous marriage. That previous marriage would continue in existence in the place where it was celebrated, effectively legalizing a form of polygamy.[10]

As we will see at the beginning of Chapter 6, other marriage restrictions have sometimes produced scenarios of this kind. They have been sufficient, even without more, to persuade courts to reject a blanket nonrecognition rule.

Defenders of the blanket rule of nonrecognition have never attempted to defend these results, probably because they have never thought about them. Yet events of this kind are not far-fetched. They occur with some regularity. In particular, parents trying to evade their child support obligations are depressingly familiar in family courts.

Objections from Federalism

The second problem with a blanket nonrecognition rule is that it is probably unconstitutional. It violates states' obligations to one another within the federal system. *Lemmon* is a bad precedent. It makes us want to cheer, of course, because it led to the freeing of slaves. But this is because we no longer believe in a federalist solution to the slavery question. Jonathan Lemmon, we think, was not entitled to own slaves anywhere. This, however, is not what the case says. Its actual reasoning, which effectively made interstate migration with their property impossible for many slaveholders, didn't make sense in a federal system. Slavery was sanctioned and protected in the original Constitution.[11]

Obstacles to interstate commerce have repeatedly been invalidated by the Supreme Court. *Lemmon* would probably have been overruled on the same basis had the Civil War not intervened. At a minimum, New York might have been required to respect the slave property of transients.[12] Unpublished notes in the papers of Chief Justice Roger B. Taney indicate that when the war broke out, he may already have been preparing to write an opinion vindicating the "obligation of all to respect the institution of slavery."[13]

Interstate commerce has been protected even in mundane cases. The Supreme Court once struck down an Illinois law that required trucks to use curved mudguards behind their tires. All of the neighboring states permitted straight mudguards, and one other state made curved mudguards illegal. The upshot was that trucks would have to either avoid Illinois or stop at the border to change their mudguards. Illinois had a legitimate interest in regulating trucks on its own roads, of course. But it couldn't enforce those regulations if the effect would be to impede the shipping of goods across state lines.[14] If differential mudguard rules are too great an obstacle to interstate commerce, so is a rule depriving a person of the protections of marriage as the price of crossing state lines.

A related federalism issue arises out of the constitutional right to travel. As one Supreme Court decision put it as early as 1868, "We are all citizens of the United States, and as members of the same community must have the right to pass and repass through every part of it without interruption, as freely as in our own States."[15] On this basis, the Court invalidated a one dollar tax on people who wanted to leave a state. If this is impermissible, then a fortiori the right to travel precludes the much heavier burden of dissolving one's closest family relations as the price of interstate travel.

Objections from Equal Protection

The third difficulty of the blanket recognition rule is that it violates equal protection and thus is unconstitutional in yet another way.

The Fourteenth Amendment provides, in relevant part, that no state shall "deny to any person within its jurisdiction the equal protection of the laws."[16] It was on this basis that the Supreme Court invalidated segregated schools and laws against interracial marriage. The Court's two most recent gay rights decisions suggest that a blanket rule of nonrecognition, of the kind authorized by DOMA, would probably be unconstitutional for similar reasons.

Romer v. Evans[17] struck down an amendment to the Colorado constitution (referred to on the ballot as Amendment 2) which provided that neither the state nor any of its subdivisions could prohibit discrimination on the basis of "homosexual, lesbian or bisexual orientation, conduct, practices or relationships."[18] The amendment, Justice Anthony Kennedy's opinion for the Court observed, "has the peculiar property of imposing a broad and undifferentiated disability on a single named group."[19] The amendment seemed to deprive gays and lesbians "even of the protection of general laws and policies that prohibit arbitrary discrimination in governmental and private settings."[20] The Court concluded that "Amendment 2 classifies homosexuals not to further a proper legislative end but to make them unequal to everyone else."[21] The broad disability imposed on a targeted group "raise[d] the inevitable inference that the disadvantage imposed is born of animosity toward the class of persons affected. '[I]f the constitutional concept of "equal protection of the laws" means anything, it must at the very least mean that a bare . . . desire to harm a politically unpopular group cannot constitute a *legitimate* governmental interest.'"[22] *Romer*'s holding may thus be summarized: If a law targets a narrowly defined group and then imposes upon it disabilities that are so broad and undifferentiated as to bear no discernible relationship to any legitimate governmental interest, then the Court will infer that the law's purpose is simply to harm that group, and so will invalidate the law.[23]

Seven years later, in *Lawrence v. Texas*,[24] the Supreme Court invalidated a law that criminalized homosexual sex. The Court held that the statute "furthers no legitimate state interest which can justify its intrusion into the personal and private life of the individual."[25] The Court relied on *Romer* to hold that the precedent of *Bowers v. Hardwick,* which had held sodomy unprotected by the right to privacy, had "sustained serious erosion."[26] The Court did not explain just how *Romer* eroded *Hardwick.* A fuller explanation appeared in Justice Sandra Day O'Connor's concurrence. O'Connor would have invalidated the Texas law under the equal protection clause, arguing that it, like the law in *Romer,* exhibits "a desire to harm a politically unpopular group."[27] Quoting *Romer,* she concluded that the Texas statute "raise[s] the inevitable inference that the disadvantage imposed is born of animosity toward the class of persons affected."[28] The majority did not expressly embrace O'Connor's equal protection theory, but it did declare it to be "a tenable argument."[29]

Part of what troubled the Court in *Lawrence* was the fact that sodomy laws singling out gays are a fairly recent development in the law, only arising in the 1970s.[30] Similarly in *Romer,* the Court was troubled that the challenged disqualification "is unprecedented in our jurisprudence," and it declared that "[i]t is not within our constitutional tradition to enact laws of this sort."[31] Extraordinary burdens, it appears, arouse suspicion. And the more unusual the burden, the more likely it is that the law will be held unconstitutional.

Together, *Lawrence* and *Romer* establish a fairly clear rule: If a law singles out gays for unprecedentedly harsh treatment, the Court will presume that what is going on is a bare desire to harm, rather than mere moral disapproval.[32] In both cases, the statute in question singled out gays for extraordinarily harsh treatment. This is what blanket nonrecognition would do, too. There has never been a blanket nonrecognition rule for any disfavored type of foreign marriage—not even interracial marriage. It follows that a blanket nonrecognition rule would be unconstitutional here as well.

This reasoning provokes an obvious objection. Not all antigay legislation, not even legislation that severely disadvantages gays, is the result of hostility and a bare desire to harm an unpopular group. Justice Antonin Scalia thought that, far from manifesting a bare desire to harm gays, the law struck down in *Romer* was "a modest attempt by seemingly tolerant Coloradans to preserve traditional sexual mores against the efforts of a politically powerful minority to revise those mores through use of the laws."[33] "Of course it is our moral heritage that one should not hate any human being or class of human beings," he continued. "But I had thought that one could consider certain conduct reprehensible—murder, for example, or polygamy, or cruelty to animals—and could exhibit even 'animus' toward such conduct. Surely that is the only sort of 'animus' at issue here: moral disapproval of homosexual conduct."[34] The inference of impermissible motive, he thought, was therefore uncalled for. The Court's opinion "disparaging as bigotry adherence to traditional attitudes," Scalia concluded, was "nothing short of insulting."[35]

Scalia is half right. The problem, as we saw in Chapter 4, is that laws that discriminate against gays often *both* express moral disapproval *and* reflect a desire to harm an unpopular group. Opposition to gay rights is a complex combination of serious moral disagreement and vicious prejudice.

Romer and *Lawrence* together establish that the more unusual the burden a law imposes on gays, the more likely it is that the law will be held unconstitutional. Traditional moralists will object that this presumption is unfair. If one thinks one's moral views correct, changing circumstances may require that one pursue those moral views through novel means. The novelty of the means, one might reasonably argue, should not automatically entail a presumption of bad motive. Some contemporary antigay rules are unprecedented, but the emergence of an active, widespread gay rights movement is also unprecedented. A prohibition such as the Texas law that singles out homosexual sex, invalidated in *Lawrence,* is one possible response to that movement. The Texas law could be, and was, supported by people of goodwill who do not question the equal dignity of gay people.[36]

The answer to this objection is that every constitutional presumption has a price and will surely impair some legitimate government interest. The presumption of innocence means that some guilty people will go free. A rule that the state may not discriminate on the basis of race will sometimes prevent the state from pursuing legitimate ends.[37] A strong First Amendment will protect some worthless and harmful speech.[38] If those rules are not unfair, neither is this one. But the concern about unfairness to conservative views takes us to the final argument against blanket nonrecognition of same-sex marriages.

The Best Argument against Same-Sex Marriage

There is a fourth, and perhaps it is the deepest, reason why *Lemmon* is a poor precedent to rely on in the same-sex marriage controversy. The conservative argument against same-sex marriage, in its most thoughtful and humane form, does not entail a blanket rule of nonrecognition.

The conservative position has changed over time. Almost no conservatives are willing today to support the kind of result that the court reached in the *Kaufmann* case considered in Chapter 1, when an inheritance was voided because a gay man was trying to leave his estate to his partner. Few conservatives want to use the law to stamp out same-sex relationships as if they were the moral equivalent of slavery. They just don't want such relationships to be given the special treatment that is given to heterosexual marriages.

Consider once more the conclusion of Chapter 4: states with strong public policies against same-sex marriage are entitled to refrain from endorsing such marriages. But this entitlement does not mean that there are no limits to what states may do to same-sex couples. The best argument against same-sex marriage is a moral argument that is not animated by hatred but that merely seeks to maintain the marital forms that are consistent with most citizens' values.

This position justifies a state in refusing to recognize same-sex marriages entered into by its own domiciliaries. It does not, however, justify blanket nonrecognition. The state does not have a legitimate interest in regulating the consensual relationships of citizens of other states. Less crude rules can fully vindicate the state's interests. We now turn to the question of what those rules should look like.

VI
Choice of Law Rules:
The Options

Kathleen Lawson married Nawal Baindail in England in 1939. Kathleen was English; Nawal was from British India. Some time after the marriage, Kathleen discovered that Nawal had previously contracted a Hindu marriage in India—"a fact in his personal history," one of the judges on appeal dryly noted, "which he did not think it necessary to reveal."[1] In 1928, he had married a woman whom the case report describes only as "a daughter of one Ramchandra,"[2] and she had borne him a son.

Kathleen sought to annul her marriage on grounds of bigamy. Nawal resisted the suit, probably because Kathleen had some money and he wanted to preserve his claim to it. Nawal cited several cases that seemed to indicate that potentially polygamous marriages were not regarded as marriages at all by English law and argued that he was therefore legally a single man at the time of his English marriage.

There was substantial authority supporting Nawal's view that his prior marriage had no effects under British law. The first British polygamy case, *Hyde v. Hyde*,[3] postulated that "marriage, as understood in Christendom, may for this purpose be defined as the voluntary union for life of one man and one woman, to the exclusion of all others,"[4] and inferred that in places that recognized polygamy, "the relation there existing between men and women is not the relation which in Christendom we recognize and intend by the words 'husband' or 'wife,' but another and altogether different relation."[5] *Hyde* was relied on in *In re Bethell*[6] to deny an inheritance to the child of a potentially polygamous marriage that an Englishman had contracted in Africa. The marriage, the court held, "was not a valid marriage according to the law of *England*."[7] *Bethell* was widely understood to mean that "polygamous marriages are wholly unrecognized by English law for any purpose whatever, even if they are only potentially polygamous."[8]

This rule was criticized, however, implying as it does that English courts "should absolutely ignore all family relations among the great majority of the human race, treating all wives among them as mere concubines, all children as bastards, and all property left by an intestate among them as escheating or becoming ownerless."[9] It was particularly anomalous because, in the days of the British empire, the technically foreign law was often the settled rule in large parts of the British dominions.[10] For this reason, *Bethell* was gradually eroded by later decisions and has now been legislatively overruled.[11]

The present English rule substantially resembles that of the *Ross* case, discussed in Chapter 3: the forbidden marriages may not take place within the forum, and people who live in England may not contract such marriages elsewhere, but polygamous marriages are otherwise recognized by English courts. Moreover, Britain evidently does not seek to interfere with the domestic relations of immigrant polygamous households.[12] Today, the British courts will almost always recognize polygamous marriages unless those marriages are celebrated in England or either party lives in England at the time of the marriage.[13]

Baindail v. Baindail was a crucial step in the erosion of *Bethell*'s blanket rule of nonrecognition. One appellate judge in *Baindail* conceded that this was "a question which is not covered by authority" but found conclusive the prospect that, if it adopted the husband's argument, "this English lady would find herself compelled in India [should he choose to return there] either to leave her husband or to share him with his Indian wife." Under these circumstances, "effect must be given to common sense and decency."[14] The annulment was granted.[15]

The *Baindail* case shows the absurdity of a rule that an otherwise valid existing marriage can wink out of existence when a person enters a state (and perhaps wink back into existence when he or she leaves?). The consequence would be multiple marriages and enormous uncertainty about spousal rights and inheritance. Several early American authorities, including Justice Story, worried that the prohibition of interracial marriage, if construed so broadly, could lead to the practical legalization of polygamy.[16]

England didn't want to legalize polygamy. But it didn't want to completely ignore the fact of Nawal Baindail's prior marriage in India, either. It wanted to recognize his marriage for some purposes, but not for all. This sounds strange, but it isn't. Marriage creates a large number of different legal rights. Generally, when marriage becomes an issue in litigation, only one of these rights is in question: a claim to an inheritance, or for support, or for damages in tort. A state's policy against recognition will be stronger in some of these contexts than it is in others. Another illustration may help clarify this.

Dalip Singh Bir died in California in 1945. His home was India, and he still had two wives there, Harnam Kaur and Jiwi. He had been married to both for more than fifty years. He left some money in California, but there was no will.

The administratrix of the estate asked the court for permission to divide the money equally between the two widows. The court refused. Because California law forbade polygamy, the court reasoned, only the first wife could inherit. Until some proof was offered as to which of the marriages was performed first, the money could not be distributed at all. And when it was distributed, the second wife would get nothing.

Harnam Kaur and Jiwi both appealed the decision. The appeals court reversed. The public policy, the court declared, "would apply only if decedent had attempted to cohabit with his two wives in California." It was not implicated in this case, where "only the descent of property is involved." The money was divided equally.[17]

The simple, blanket rule of nonrecognition is excessively crude. It is insufficiently attentive to the legitimate interests of the parties to same-sex marriages and of their domicile state. As *Baindail* shows, it also gives too little regard to the rights of third parties. More complex rules are unavoidable.

What would a better rule look like? Several possibilities lie between automatic recognition and blanket nonrecognition, which we have considered and rejected. Each of these would attempt to strike a balance among the individual and state interests involved, rather than simply disregarding any of them. None relies on the repugnance rationale for the public policy exception (described in Chapter 2), which turns on the forum's distaste for the substantive foreign law.

One possibility is to follow the Second Restatement rule (and some of the miscegenation cases) by holding that a marriage valid under the law of the most interested state at the time of the marriage is thereafter valid everywhere, even if the parties later move to a state where that marriage could not have been entered into. Second, one could hold that the legal right of two people to be married to each other is to be determined on the basis of the law of the common domicile from time to time. Third, one could say that the interests of the different jurisdictions are to be balanced on a case-by-case basis, in order to establish which of them has a greater interest in determining the existence or nonexistence of the marriage with respect to the incident of marriage that is at issue in the litigation. Finally, one can use the Second Restatement's approach to decide whether a valid marriage exists, but use the domicile state's law to determine what incidents of marriage the couple may enjoy.

Settling It Once and for All

A solution that would settle the status of a marriage once and for all is that of the Second Restatement, in which a marriage valid where celebrated is valid everywhere "unless it violates the strong public policy of another state which had the most significant relationship to the spouses and the marriage at the time of the marriage."[18] The Restatement is the basis of choice of law in approximately half the states.[19]

The Restatement is the culmination of a long trend toward the erosion of the public policy exception. The modern tendency may be illustrated briefly by examining twentieth century efforts to codify prevailing American law.

In 1912, the Uniform Marriage Evasion Act sought to codify the rule nullifying out-of-state marriages by domiciliaries whose marriage would be prohibited within the domicile. Only five states adopted it before it was withdrawn in 1943 because of its limited adoption.[20] In 1934, the first Restatement of Conflict of Laws similarly held that a marriage "which is against the law of the state of domicil of either party, though the requirements of the law of the state of celebration have been complied with, will be invalid everywhere" in cases of polygamy, incest as defined by the domicile, "marriage between persons of different races where such marriages are at the domicil regarded as odious," or other marriages governed by evasion statutes.[21] In 1971, the Restatement (Second) of Conflict of Laws made this rule less stringent, providing that, in order for its strong public policy to void a marriage, a state must have "the most significant relationship to the spouses and the marriage at the time of the marriage."[22] Since it disregarded the law of the place of celebration only in cases where the place where the marriage was centered had the most significant relationship to the marriage, the Restatement's public policy exception would seem to have relied upon what, in Chapter 2, we called the legitimate-interest rationale for the rule. Moreover, it even limited the domicile state's interest by requiring that it have the most significant relationship with the parties *at the time of the marriage.* A concession was thus made to policies against evasion, but parties once validly married were married always and forever, even if they took up residence in a jurisdiction that would not have permitted them to marry.[23] At about the same time, the Uniform Marriage and Divorce Act completed the codifiers' war on the exception by validating all marriages that were valid where celebrated and doing away with the public policy exception altogether.[24]

As noted already, the kind of solution offered by the Second Restatement was considered and rejected by some southern courts during the Jim Crow era because it meant that they would have to allow some interracial cohabitation within their borders. In the present context, this solution would mean that same-sex couples could not marry on a weekend trip to Massachusetts and expect their marriage to be recognized in Georgia, but they could move to Massachusetts, marry while living there, and after a few years return to Georgia and demand recognition.

The resulting legal regime would resemble the present English rule with respect to polygamy. The disfavored form of marriage could not validly be celebrated in the forum state, and domiciliaries of the forum could not enter into that sort of marriage anywhere. Otherwise, however, such marriages will ordinarily be recognized for all purposes, even if the parties to the marriages permanently immigrate into the forum state.

While this approach honors state interests as much as possible while avoiding redeterminations of a marriage's validity, some states are likely to insist that they need more than this if they are to vindicate their domestic policies. If a state has a strong public policy against same-sex marriage, then this must mean that it does not want a same-sex couple living permanently as a married couple within its borders. This policy would apply regardless of where the marriage in question came into existence. If a state's own domiciliaries are forbidden to live in same-sex marriages, then the same constraint can sensibly be imposed on those who voluntarily immigrate. A state could reasonably conclude that it would be unfair to have recent arrivals enjoy benefits that are denied to long-term residents.

There is one last argument for recognition of immigrant marriages, even in those states with declared public policies against same-sex marriage. As already noted, the Jim Crow courts were evenly split on the question of whether interracial marriages must be recognized in immigration situations. Since that time, the presumption in favor of recognizing marriages has plainly become stronger than it was in the 1800s. This strengthened presumption, one might argue, serves as a tie-breaker in the face of evenly divided nineteenth-century authority. There is, however, another equally plausible alternate explanation for the shift in the modern tendency toward blanket recognition: the weakening, throughout the twentieth century, of public policies against certain kinds of marriage. Perhaps the presumption in favor of marriage has grown stronger, but it is also possible that the countervailing policies became weaker—until the advent of same-sex marriage.

Domicile-Based Rules

Douglas Laycock has suggested that a clean solution to the question of a marriage's existence would be to rely, in all cases, on the law of the parties' domicile:

> A sophisticated territorialism would recognize that often the law's purpose is to regulate a relationship among a group of people, and that the particular event that caused a dispute within the relationship is incidental to the larger relationship and the regulatory scheme that governs it. A continuing relationship requires stable regulation under a single law, even if there is an element of legal fiction in locating the relationship. Most obviously, the relationship

of a husband and wife is sensibly located in their common home state, and that law should govern even when they travel abroad or invest in property abroad. The common home state has by far the greatest interest in regulating relationships formed there; such domicile-based choice of law rules impose no disadvantage on citizens of sister states; and it is perfectly sound to reify the relationship and locate it at home. If one spouse moves to a new state, that unilateral act cannot change the law governing the relationship; the law of the original common home state should continue to govern until and unless both spouses move elsewhere.[25]

This solution preserves states' ability to govern the status of their own domiciliaries while entitling citizens to travel without constant, confusing changes in their legal status. If both same-sex spouses move to another state, their marriage would cease (or, perhaps, become dormant; it is unclear whether it should spring back to life when they, or one of them, moves back to the state in which they were married). As long as they make their home in a state that recognizes same-sex marriage, however, they would have to be recognized as married everywhere and for all purposes.

This solution is not without its problems. "Domicile" is a category with fuzzy boundaries of its own; it is not always clear how one determines whether a person has changed domicile.[26] And it is not clear how Laycock would address cases, increasingly common, in which the spouses live in different states at the time the marriage is celebrated.[27] Clearcut, codified rules of domicile would help. For example, one could deem the situs of the marriage to be the last place (if any) where the parties lived together for a year.

This approach would also, as a practical matter, call for some procedure for formally nullifying a same-sex marriage when one or both of the parties have left the state recognizing it. If a member of a same-sex couple leaves Massachusetts, for example, and later wants to marry a person of the opposite sex in Louisiana, he or she should be required to secure a formal declaration that the first marriage no longer exists. Otherwise, the marital status of the spouse who remains in Massachusetts would be doubtful.

Finally, if the marriage just dissolves with a move to a new state, some court somewhere must be able to divide the property, adjudicate custody of any children, and so forth. Perhaps the former domicile ought to retain continuing jurisdiction for that purpose.

A domicile-based solution accommodates states' interests in not having their domestic institutions governed by another state's laws. It generates predictable, nonarbitrary results. It offers a federalist solution to a profound moral disagreement. But it doesn't handle transitions well. It has no good account of what happens when people change domiciles. For that reason, it may end up licensing evasion of family obligations. We need to turn to a different approach.

Different Incidents, Different Outcomes

Many courts and scholars would allow the choice of law in any particular case to depend on which incident of marriage is at issue. One major treatise observes that "the significance of a person's status and its relevance arises in conflict-of-laws litigation almost exclusively concerning questions regarding the incidents of the relationship, such as succession or claim to property, or a claim for support, or a claim for damages in tort."[28] Moreover, "in recent choice of law cases, the courts have begun to recognize that the enjoyment of different incidents of marriage involves different policies."[29] As we saw in Chapter 3, some of the miscegenation cases anticipated this approach: foreign interracial marriages were recognized where the couple did not seek to cohabit within the state.

It has been a cliché among scholars of property law that property is not a single thing but a "bundle of rights" that are not necessarily tied together.[30] The association together of the various rights of property is historically contingent, and in some cases it makes sense to unbundle them. I own my car; I am entitled to exclusive possession of it, and I can sell it if I like. My heart is also mine, but the law won't let me sell it. Different parts of the bundle reflect different policies.

Similarly, marriage can be regarded as a "bundle of inci-dents."[31] They may generally go together, but there may in par-ticular cases be good reason to separate them out.[32] Recall the argument in Chapter 4 that the debate about same-sex mar-riage is really two debates, normative and administrative, and that there is value in separating them from one another. The "incidents approach" attempts to do just this: to consider the administrative question without resolving the normative one.

This approach will call for recognition even in some eva-sion cases. The leading case is *In re Estate of Lenherr*.[33] In 1930, Leo Lenherr was divorced from his wife in Pennsylvania on grounds of adultery. That same year, Sarah Barney was divorced from her husband on the same basis. Each was named as co-respondent in the other's adultery trial. Under Pennsylvania law, a former spouse who had been divorced on grounds of adultery could not marry, during the life of the former spouse, the person with whom the adultery was committed. In 1932, after the divorce decrees were entered but while the former spouses were still living, Leo and Sarah were married in West Virginia and returned to Pennsylvania, where they lived as husband and wife until Leo died in 1971.

The issue was whether the state could subject Sarah's inheritance to a transfer tax—a tax from which spouses were exempt. The Supreme Court of Pennsylvania held that, for this purpose, the ban on remarriage after divorce did not apply. That prohibition, the court held, "is intended not so much as a penalty on the parties who failed to recognize the sanctity of the former marriage vow as it is intended to protect the sensibilities of the injured spouse."[34] Denying the tax exemption would neither reduce the affront to the former spouse nor deter the adultery or subsequent remarriage. It would, however, have the unjust result of ignoring the fact that joint marital property "is in reality the product of their joint efforts and should pass to the survivor without the imposition of a tax."[35] The marriage was recognized for the limited purpose of upholding the tax exemption.

The trouble with this approach is its inherent uncertainty. It is hard for parties to anticipate how their enjoyment of any particular incident of their marriage will be weighed against countervailing policies. Marriage carries with it a huge array of incidents. In a famous study, the federal General Accounting Office conducted a study of the U.S. Code to determine how many federal rights and responsibilities depended on whether one was married. It found more than a thousand federal statutes in which marital status was a factor[36]—and only federal rights were being counted. A very broad range of marital rights and responsibilities arise out of state law, concerning family dissolution, adoption, domestic violence, liability for family expenses, taxation, health-care decision making, inheritance, the right to sue for wrongful death, eligibility for welfare benefits, health insurance, and homestead rights (which protect a home from forced sale by creditors).[37]

Barbara Cox has argued that it would be unacceptably burdensome to require same-sex couples to "relitigate their marital status repeatedly as they request recognition of their marriage for each incident."[38] Deborah Henson has pointed out, on the other hand, that treating each incident separately may result in recognition of more same-sex marriages, for more purposes, than would occur if courts had to decide marriage recognition issues wholesale.[39] A public policy is less likely to be offended by limited recognition of a marriage, for limited purposes, than by a judicial declaration that the marriage is valid for all purposes.[40] Nonetheless, the inevitable consequence of this approach, as one of its most prominent proponents conceded, is "a situation where a marriage may be good for the purposes of one issue and yet invalid for the purposes of another."[41]

Cox and Henson are both right. If the argument of this book is correct, then ordinary choice of law analysis should continue to govern these issues. The incidents approach should remain available to litigators, while the other approaches will be of interest primarily to legislators, although state supreme court judges may wish to craft more predictable rules if legislators do not act.

The strongest case for the incidents approach focuses on the puzzle presented in the *Baindail* case described at the beginning of this chapter. If a certain kind of marriage is prohibited in the forum, is a person who has contracted a marriage of that kind elsewhere a single person in the forum, and so free to contract a new marriage with someone else? If a prior same-sex marriage is going to be an impediment to remarriage in, say, Georgia, and yet Georgia is not going to recognize in every respect the same-sex marriages of those who relocate from Massachusetts, then there is no alternative to disaggregation of the incidents of marriage. Georgia would have to say that the Massachusetts marriage is valid as an impediment to a subsequent remarriage but invalid for purposes of, for example, filing a joint state tax return.

A Synthesis

It may be possible to synthesize the different approaches in a way that preserves the strengths of each while avoiding their weaknesses. Uniform recognition gives too little weight to states' strong public policies against recognition. Blanket non-recognition recognizes the importance of territorial boundaries but produces such arbitrary and unfair results that it is probably unconstitutional. The Second Restatement prevents the marriage validity question from being repeatedly reconsidered but arguably gives inadequate weight to the public policies of states that do not want same-sex couples cohabiting as married within their borders. Laycock produces clear rules for the most part that give due weight to each state's interests but does not adequately account for the need to formally terminate marriages. And the incidents approach balances the relevant issues in a way that takes full account of the equities in each case but seems ad hoc and unpredictable. The solution, I suggest, is to recast Laycock as a systematizer of incidents and the Restatement as determining merely which marriages are valid ab initio.

With respect to whether a marriage exists at all or is void for all purposes, the Restatement's rule makes sense: a marriage valid where celebrated is valid everywhere unless it violates the strong public policy (which means, in practice, the marriage evasion statute or mini-DOMA) of the state where the parties are domiciled before and immediately after the marriage. Absent the operation of this exception, a marriage exists and, until formal divorce or annulment, is an impediment to any subsequent marriage by either of the parties, regardless of any later change of domicile by either.

Each state's own public policies will determine whether its own domiciliaries (including immigrants) who have entered into same-sex marriages may enjoy the incidents of those marriages, such as a homestead exemption, the right to file a joint state tax return, or the ability to compel an unwilling employer to insure one's spouse. And, as we will see, the analysis will be different with different incidents of marriage. Some, but not all, of them may be able to be recognized under some rubric other than "marriage."

It is otherwise with domiciliaries of other states who are merely passing through. If a Massachusetts resident visiting Michigan is killed by a drunk driver there, the surviving same-sex spouse should have the right to file a wrongful death suit. Unless the couple lives within its borders, no state has a sufficient interest in an extraterritorially valid same-sex marriage to deny it recognition.

We now must consider how this approach would play out in specific applications.

VII

When to (and When Not to) Recognize Same-Sex Marriages

Neal Conrad Spicehandler was having a good day. He and his partner, John Langan, had lately celebrated their civil union in Vermont and just that morning had bought a house together in New York, where they lived. He was a healthy forty-one-year-old, and the future looked good.

But the next day he was dead. What killed him was a series of bizarre accidents, of a kind that no one could have anticipated. He happened to be walking on the street when Ronald Popadich, a diagnosed paranoid schizophrenic, was on an enraged homicidal spree. In the space of a few days in February 2002, Popadich shot two people, one of whom died, and went driving wildly through Manhattan, running down pedestrians at random. He injured twenty-five people, including Conrad. Popadich later told police that he wanted to kill as many people as possible.[1]

Conrad was taken to St. Vincent's hospital and underwent two surgeries for a broken leg. He was in a lot of pain from the compound fracture but was in good spirits nonetheless. Before the second surgery, he was telling jokes to friends and family members in his hospital room. The injury was not thought to be life-threatening. But he evidently was concerned enough to write his partner John a note on his way into the operating room:

> John:
> I'm going under. I haven't had a chance to see you.
> I love you.
> I've made my life in your heart.
> Conrad[2]

Early the next morning, he died in the hospital of an embolus of unknown origin.[3]

Conrad and John had been in a relationship for fifteen years, since 1986, and had lived together for most of that time. They had entered into a civil union in Vermont four months after that state began to make them available, at a ceremony attended by forty family members and friends. They participated together in family functions. And as mentioned above, on the day of the accident, they had just purchased a house.

Since broken legs don't usually kill people, John investigated whether the hospital might be at fault and ended up suing it for medical malpractice. John's right to sue the hospital depended on whether he was Conrad's "spouse" under New York law. Lawsuits for wrongful death are brought by the estate of the person who has died. Such suits did not exist at common law, however, and the wrongful death statutes that authorize them typically designate certain family members who can recover. A person has to be one of that named group in order to be able to sue.[4] A spouse can sue for wrongful death; a friend can't. So John could sue if and only if New York law recognized him as Conrad's spouse.

The trial judge held that the case could proceed. An earlier court decision had established that a same-sex partner could not recover for wrongful death. That case, however, had not involved a relationship that was treated as a marriage by a sister state. New York is willing to recognize some foreign marriages, such as common law marriages, that are not valid under its own laws. There was no strong public policy against same-sex marriage in New York. Notably, New York had not enacted a mini-DOMA. The fact that the civil union was technically an evasive one evidently was not a problem. The judge also thought that denying same-sex couples rights given to other foreign married couples might violate equal protection. The concern that underlay the earlier denial of a partner's right to sue, "orderly succession of property rights among clearly defined classes of persons," was not implicated here: "There cannot be two spouses making claims under Vermont law, as there could be with couples who may separate and combine at will."[5]

The Appellate Division reversed, in a 3–2 split decision. It relied on the plain language of the wrongful death statute, which limited recovery to a spouse, noting that "[t]he fact that . . . the State of Massachusetts has judicially created [the right to same-sex marriage] is of no moment here since the plaintiff and the decedent were not married in that jurisdiction."[6] The Vermont Supreme Court had not equated civil unions with heterosexual marriage. The dissenters agreed with the majority's reading of the statute but held that the exclusion was an unconstitutional denial of equal protection. The clear implication of all of the opinions was that the result would have been different if the couple had been married in Massachusetts. The judges evidently thought it decisive that Vermont didn't regard the relationship as a marriage, but, for reasons that should now be familiar, this was the wrong question to ask. Having decided that Vermont law was applicable, the court should then have asked, what would Vermont do in this situation? The precise issue was whether Vermont law treated John as a spouse for purposes of filing a wrongful death action. Had the judges asked the right question, they would have come out the other way. The case is being appealed.

But what if there were a strong public policy in New York rejecting same-sex marriage? Forty states have laws on the books declaring that they will not recognize foreign same-sex marriages and that such marriages are against their public policy.[7] They present a significant obstacle to the recognition of same-sex marriages from Massachusetts and any other states that may allow them in the future. (It is less clear whether most are even relevant to the recognition of civil unions from other states because most of them use the word "marriage" to describe what they are denying to same-sex couples.) Some of them have very strong language, describing same-sex marriages as "void" or "prohibited." The miscegenation cases indicate that this language does not enact a blanket nonrecognition rule; the extraterritorial miscegenation cases described in Chapter 3 involved statutes with equally strong language but recognized the marriages in question. Yet as we saw, those cases did not work out entirely coherent rules of law that provided for all the contingencies that might arise. They offer incomplete guidance.

A more nuanced set of rules would draw the distinctions that the miscegenation cases approached but did not quite reach. There are four relevant types of case: evasive, migratory, visitor, and extraterritorial. Each requires a different analysis.

(It makes no difference whether the same-sex marriage in question was celebrated in another state or in another country, such as Canada.)

The first category, *evasive marriages*,[8] includes cases in which parties have traveled out of their home state for the express purpose of evading that state's prohibition of their marriages and thereafter immediately returned home. Such marriages usually will be invalid if they violate the strong public policy of the couple's home state.

The second category, *migratory marriages*, includes cases in which the parties contracted a marriage that was valid where they lived and subsequently moved to a state where their marriage was prohibited. These situations will present complicated issues, even if (as is now the case in forty states) there is a statute denying recognition to foreign same-sex marriages. Property claims arising out of a marriage cannot be simply annulled by the decision of one spouse to move to another state. A same-sex marriage has to be an impediment to the remarriage of either of the partners: they can't just take on a second spouse in another state. Even the states most opposed to same-sex marriage never wanted to legalize polygamy. Moreover, if the incident of marriage in question is one that could have been conferred by contract under the forum's law, such as the right to make medical decisions for one's partner, then the state's policy cannot be offended by the mere fact that the couple took advantage of a legal shortcut to that right created by another state's law. More generally, if an incident can be characterized without reference to the marriage—if it can be called a "parental right" or a "right to enforce a judgment"—then it should be recognized as such.

The third category, and the one that most urgently demands clarity, is *visitor marriages*, in which a couple or a member of a couple is temporarily present in a state that does not recognize their marriage. Though little authority addresses this precise question, such marriages should always be recognized, for all purposes. Any other result is inconsistent with the constitutional right of citizens to travel.

The fourth category is *extraterritorial cases.* Here the parties have never lived within a state that forbids same-sex marriage, but the marriage is relevant to litigation conducted there. For example, after the death intestate of one spouse, the other may seek to inherit property that was located within the forum state. In these cases, there is clear authority in favor of recognition.

Evasive Marriages

The type of case that most of the discussion of same-sex marriage has focused on is the evasive marriage, in which a couple leaves a state that forbids their marriage, marries in another, and then returns to their home state. It is also the weakest case for recognition. Such marriages will be invalid if they violate the strong public policy of the couple's home state. The basic idea, as we saw in Chapter 2, is that states have the right to govern their own residents.

The evasion case is directly provided for by a law in Massachusetts which declares that marriages cannot be contracted there by people from another jurisdiction "if such marriage would be void if contracted in such other jurisdiction," and that marriages in violation of that restriction are void.[9] A challenge to that law failed in court.[10] But it makes sense to ask what the world would look like without this restriction, both because the restriction may be invalidated and because same-sex marriage may eventually be recognized in another state without an anti-evasion statute.

Discerning public policy will be easy in the forty states that have legislation on the books, enacted after 1992, declaring that other states' same-sex marriages are void or prohibited. In the other states, the outcome will be less certain. The public policy doctrine, discussed in Chapter 2, is an anomaly in the conflict of laws and is rarely invoked. Most states that nominally follow it have never used it to deny recognition to a marriage.[11]

Absent a statute, it is not clear how a public policy could be shown. It is clear that a mere difference between forum law and foreign law is not sufficient; if it were, then there could never be any conflicts analysis because forum law would always be applied. The answer depends on a close reading of state law sources. One source that might once have been helpful is the existence of a state sodomy law, but all such laws have now been declared unconstitutional and void.[12] So states without mini-DOMAs cannot be certain how evasion cases would be resolved in their courts. (If they have not passed such statutes, this suggests that they aren't very worried about this uncertainty.) The absence of such a statute was deemed highly relevant by the court in *Langan v. St. Vincent's,* discussed above, although even it was unwilling to say that same-sex marriage would be recognized for all purposes in New York. In New York and in two other states without mini-DOMAs, Connecticut and Rhode Island, the state attorneys general have opined that same-sex marriages will be recognized for some purposes.[13]

Most states do have mini-DOMA statutes, and they will generally preclude recognition in evasion cases. This is precisely what they are intended to do. Thus a Georgia court appropriately declined to recognize a Vermont civil union in a case in which both parties were Georgia domiciliaries, though the court did not notice the significance of domicile.[14] Similarly, a federal court in Florida dismissed a suit by two Florida women who had married in Massachusetts and wanted to compel recognition by Florida.[15]

Even in evasion cases, however, it is not clear whether the policy would be applied to invalidate a marriage if there were no possibility of the marriage continuing within the state's borders. The trial court in *Langan* observed that the policy behind the wrongful death statutes was to make sure that actual family members are compensated. It thus found for recognition in that case, without expressing any opinion about recognition in other cases.[16] (The Appellate Division did not disagree but reversed on other grounds.)

It is also unclear what result a court would reach in the state in which an evasive marriage is celebrated, should the marriage become the object of litigation there. Massachusetts has a statute voiding the evasive marriages celebrated there of people who come from states where their marriages are prohibited, but Connecticut, Vermont, and California do not.

The clarity of an anti-evasion rule is also limited by the fact that its application depends on the determination of the domicile of the parties at the time of the marriage, and this is not always clear. Recall from Chapter 2 that a person changes domicile if he or she moves to a different state with the intention to remain there indefinitely. It is not always clear what someone intended at an earlier time. And to the extent that it is not, it will be unclear whether a marriage is evasive and therefore void.

It is thus a mistake for states to construe mini-DOMAs to forbid courts from issuing orders dissolving evasive same-sex marriages. Courts have in fact been split on this question. Two Connecticut courts construed Connecticut law to deny them subject matter jurisdiction to dissolve or annul a Vermont civil union and a Massachusetts same-sex marriage entered into by Connecticut domiciliaries.[17] A Texas court approved a division of property between two gay men but declined to expressly dissolve their civil union.[18] On the other hand, judges in Iowa and West Virginia approved uncontested divorces between lesbians who had been in Vermont civil unions.[19]

The problem is a pressing one because Vermont courts will dissolve civil unions only for people who have lived in Vermont for at least six months, meaning that residents of other states have no access to Vermont courts.[20] Residents of other states can get into Vermont civil unions very easily, but it is hard to terminate them. If a person has entered into a civil union, that person, for the reasons just given, cannot reliably get out of it simply by moving to a state with a mini-DOMA. Because it will often be uncertain whether a marriage is evasive, the only way to be sure that a union will not have continuing legal effects is to formally end it. The ability to exit is one incident of marriage that should be available everywhere.[21] It is odd for a state to oppose same-sex marriages by making it virtually impossible for people to end them. (As this is written, there is no case law involving attempts to dissolve Massachusetts same-sex marriages in other states.)

So, to summarize, these would be the guidelines for evasive marriages:

> *Rule:* A marriage is evasive only if the parties are domiciled in the state that prohibits them from marrying. Evasive marriages will, as a general matter, not be recognized.
>
> *Exception:* Recognition will be granted in cases in which the state policy underlying the specific incident of marriage, such as inheritance or the

right to file a wrongful death suit, would be pro-
moted by recognition of the marriage, and in
which there is no possibility that the marriage
will continue to exist within the state's borders.
This exception will probably operate only in cases
in which one of the spouses has died.

Complication: It is not always obvious where someone is domiciled, so there will sometimes be
room for dispute as to whether a marriage was
in fact evasive.

Migratory Marriages

Migratory marriages are cases in which the parties did not intend to evade the law of any state when they married. Instead,
they contracted a marriage that was valid where they lived and
subsequently moved to a state where it was prohibited. An example would be a same-sex couple who lived in Massachusetts
when they married and later moved to Pennsylvania.

These are hard cases. It is clear that, absent a statutory
ban on same-sex marriage, the state's public policy will not be
clear enough to justify withholding recognition. Even if there
is such a statute, the state's interest may not be strong enough
to outweigh the couple's interest in the continuing validity of
their marriage.

The prevailing position in American law, we saw in Chapter 2, is that the mere fact of migration cannot void an originally valid marriage. But we also saw that this rule created great
difficulties in the past when it meant that the southern states
would have to tolerate some interracial cohabitation within
their borders after all. States with mini-DOMAs may be similarly distressed by the prospect of having to recognize the
marriages of migrants. They may also think it unfair to have

two classes of same-sex couples: longtime residents who cannot be in same-sex marriages, and recent arrivals who can. They may thus be tempted to adopt the blanket nonrecognition rule, which we already saw in Chapter 5 to be unworkable. Some variant of the incidents approach is unavoidable.

How can one determine whether any particular incident is available in a state with a strong public policy, stated in its statutes, against same-sex marriage? The treatment of the incidents approach in the context of miscegenation can't immediately be translated to the context of same-sex marriage because the state policies are necessarily different. The incident of marriage that was most important in the miscegenation cases was the right to sexual intercourse. The central public policy of miscegenation law was (to put it bluntly) the urgently felt imperative of keeping black penises out of white vaginas. Any state purpose of preventing sexual conduct is now mooted by the Supreme Court's decision in *Lawrence v. Texas*,[22] which held that such conduct cannot be criminalized. As argued in Chapter 4, the state's interest in the same-sex marriage case is better characterized as an interest in avoiding giving symbolic recognition to same-sex marriages as continuing relations within the state's borders. This interest is not necessarily implicated by administrative measures that do not recognize same-sex marriage as such.

Many marital rights can arise in nonmarital ways. For instance, some incidents of marriage can be conferred by contract, such as those involving inheritance or the ability of a person to make medical decisions for his or her partner. Others, however, such as the right to file a joint tax return, can be conferred only by operation of law.

If a right is one that the parties could have achieved via private contract under the forum's law, then the forum cannot coherently be said to have a public policy against them enjoying that incident. Here one choice of law rule is particularly relevant: no fundamental public policy is involved when states have different formalities regarding the formation of a contract, such as different approaches to Statute of Frauds questions (which dictate when a contract must be in writing) or laws providing that contracts are invalid if made on a Sunday.[23] If a foreign same-sex marriage simply provides, under a different formal procedure, rights that might have been conferred by forum law, then there is no public policy against enforcing those rights.[24]

So a state can simply call the foreign marriage a contract and treat it as a contract under state law.[25] The forum's policy against same-sex marriage doesn't come into play because the state need not concede that the relationship that it is recognizing is being treated as a marriage.[26]

The analysis is even more straightforward in states such as Connecticut that have civil unions that confer the rights of marriage in all but name. In these states, foreign same-sex marriages ought to be simply treated as if they were civil unions.[27]

Recognition is also appropriate if a same-sex marriage in another state has ended in divorce, and the divorce decree requires one of the former spouses to make regular payments to the other, for either alimony or child support. Suppose that one of the former spouses moves to a state that does not recognize same-sex marriage. Should that state enforce the judgment? Yes, it should. (I will postpone until Chapter 8 the very strong argument that the Constitution requires it to do so.) Since the marriage has already been dissolved, the couple is not attempting to live as cohabiting same-sex spouses within the state's borders. All the court is being asked to do is to enforce monetary obligations, which is something it does all the time. Once more, a state need not concede that a relationship is a marriage in order to give it some legal effect.

The same analysis should apply if there has been no divorce, and one spouse has simply entered the state seeking to evade financial obligations. The state does not need to tolerate same-sex marriage within its borders when it enforces such obligations. Every state should agree with what the Washington Supreme Court said in another context: "[W]e may safely assume that this state has no policy interest in maintaining within its borders a sanctuary for fleeing debtors."[28]

Finally, and very importantly, there is one set of rights and obligations that cannot be conferred by contract but that should remain undisturbed if a couple migrates into a forum. As a general matter, if rights of third parties, created by operation of state law, are involved, those third-party rights should not be voided by the unilateral decision to move. In particular, parent-child relationships should not be allowed to be dissolved in this way.[29] If a same-sex couple, or one of them, migrates to a state that does not recognize same-sex marriage, and there is a child or children to whom the pertinent adult has parental rights and obligations, those rights and obligations should persist even after migration.[30] A different rule would violate the children's constitutional right to their relationships with their parents.[31]

In other cases, this result is obvious. Consider the issue of children born as a consequence of surrogacy contracts, in which a woman is hired to bear the child of a person or couple who cannot produce a child without assistance. Some states allow such contracts; others prohibit them. Suppose a child born as a consequence of such a contract moves to a state that prohibits such contracts. Does anyone imagine that the child's new home will, or should, refuse to recognize the parent-child relationship that is already in existence and thereby nullify, for instance, a nine-year-old's relationship with one or both parents?[32]

The conservative case against same-sex marriage, we saw in Chapter 4, is centrally concerned with the protection of children. It would be bizarre and ironic for a state to harm actual children in order to make a symbolic point. The legal ties between parents and children should not be affected by any family member's decision to cross state lines. The state should ignore the existence of the same-sex marriage and just characterize the relation as one of parent and child.

To summarize what the law should be in this area:

> *Rule:* Migratory marriages are marriages in which a couple, validly married in the state where they were then domiciled, subsequently moves to a state where their marriage is not recognized. Such marriages are to be recognized as "marriages" only to the extent of being impediments to a subsequent marriage.
>
> *Exception:* Any right or obligation of marriage that can be recharacterized as a nonmarital right—such as a right to contract, or a parent-child relation, or an obligation created by a judicial judgment—should be recognized.
>
> *Exception to the exception:* Rights that are not capable of being so recharacterized, such as the right to file a joint state tax return, will not be recognized.

Visitor Marriages

Visitor marriages, in which a couple is temporarily visiting a state that does not recognize their marriage, most urgently demand clarity because they probably will arise more frequently than any of the other cases. In the United States today, nearly everyone sometimes travels across state lines, and the proportion is probably even higher in states as geographically small as Massachusetts and Vermont. Such marriages should always be recognized.

Recall from Chapter 3 that, in *Ex parte Kinney*,[33] a federal court declared in 1879 that a member of an interracial marriage would "have a right of transit with his wife through Virginia, and of temporary stoppage, and of carrying on any business here not requiring residence." The reasoning of *Kinney* is a fairly straightforward application of principles of federalism. As pointed out in Chapter 5, it is well settled that there is a constitutional right to travel and that "all citizens of the United States . . . must have the right to pass and repass through every part of it without interruption."[34] The marriages of visitors should always be recognized, for all purposes.

In practice, the analysis will not often differ from that in the migratory cases because most of the rights of marriage that cannot be conferred by contract are usually asserted in the state of one's domicile. State taxes, for example, are usually imposed on domiciliaries. Usually, but not always: some people cross state lines when they commute to work, and the jurisdiction where they work can tax their income. If a person from Connecticut who is in a civil union there works in New York City, then New York can tax the income earned there. Since the person is a visitor from Connecticut, the marriage should be recognized for purposes of computing his or her tax deductions.

There is admittedly something strange about this result. For instance, a Connecticut woman in a civil union gets to take a deduction on a New York tax return, but if she moves to New York, she loses the deduction. The claim of the Connecticut native seems no stronger than that of the person from New

York: particularly if she had the New York job before the civil union was entered into, she can't even claim to be unfairly surprised by the operation of New York law, as many visitors could.[35] This is the unavoidable consequence of making results turn on domicile, as the law has tended to do in this area. The cost of having clear legal tests is that there will be cases on opposite sides of the line that look a lot like one another.

In sum:

> *Rule:* The marriages of visitors should be recognized for all purposes, regardless of the public policy of the forum state.

Extraterritorial Marriages

Extraterritorial marriages are those in which the parties have never lived within the state, but in which the marriage is relevant to litigation conducted there. For example, after the death intestate of one spouse, the other may seek to inherit property that was located within the forum state. That was the issue in *Miller v. Lucks,* discussed in Chapter 3.

On this question the case law is unanimous. In the miscegenation cases, these marriages were routinely upheld. If public policy was not enough to prevent recognition then, it should not be now, either. Again, the rule should be simple:

> *Rule:* Same-sex marriages in which the parties have never lived within the state should be recognized for all purposes, regardless of the public policy of the forum state.

Thus far there is little case law on recognition of foreign civil unions, and all of the cases involve evasive marriages. The question of migratory, visitor, or extraterritorial marriages has not yet arisen.

The cases that are likely to be most troublesome for states that disfavor same-sex marriage will involve visitor marriages because they have a strong claim to recognition for all purposes and, unlike extraterritorial cases, they are likely to arise often. The constitutional and other legal arguments for recognition have already been discussed. People with moral objections to homosexual conduct may also want to contemplate one other consideration. The story of Sodom in the book of Genesis is often taken to be a categorical condemnation of homosexual conduct,[36] but it is equally a condemnation of inhospitality toward visitors. States that are transfixed by one danger should not thoughtlessly fall into the other.

VIII

The Irrelevance of Full Faith and Credit and the Defense of Marriage Act

Janet and Lisa Miller-Jenkins, who were then living in Virginia, formed a civil union in Vermont in 2000. Lisa gave birth to Isabella, conceived through artificial insemination, in 2002. They moved to Vermont when Isabella was two months old. Janet and Lisa shared parental responsibility. "After Lisa nursed her, my duty was to get her to go to sleep, and I'd put her on my heartbeat and, boom, she'd go to sleep," Janet said.

When Lisa tried to have a second child and had a miscarriage, "it was like a black cloud over the house," Janet said. In September 2003, Lisa decided to move back to Virginia to be near her family. She wanted to end the relationship and filed to dissolve her civil union in a Vermont court. Her attorney waived the right to challenge Janet's parentage, requested that Janet pay Lisa child support, and asked the judge to determine a visitation and custody arrangement. After the judge granted Janet temporary joint custody, Lisa switched attorneys and filed another suit in Virginia.[1] She refused to allow Janet visitation, and a Vermont judge held her in contempt in September 2004.[2]

In October 2004, a Virginia judge ruled that Janet had no parental rights. Janet, he wrote in an earlier order, "cannot claim a right to legal custody under the laws of this Commonwealth as her claims are based on rights under Vermont's civil union laws that are null and void" under Virginia law.

Shortly thereafter, Lisa was held in contempt by the Vermont court for violating its custody order, and Janet is now seeking full custody in that state.[3]

Which state's law should apply—Vermont's or Virginia's? If this were not a same-sex couple, the answer would be clear. The federal Parental Kidnapping Prevention Act (PKPA) holds that, when custody is already being considered in one state, no other state can consider the matter. Under PKPA, the case would have to stay in Vermont where it began. And a Vermont court would certainly apply Vermont law. Congress enacted PKPA because this type of situation had become depressingly familiar: in child custody disputes, the noncustodial parent would sometimes snatch the child, travel to another state, and there file a new custody proceeding. Courts in the new state would often reward this misbehavior by ignoring the other state's custody determination and making a new one. PKPA was intended to put a stop to that.

In the Miller-Jenkins litigation, Janet argued that the Virginia court was barred from reopening the custody question by PKPA, which provides that states (except in special circumstances not relevant here) "shall not modify . . . any custody determination or visitation determination made consistently with the provisions of this section by a court of another State."[4] But Lisa responded that PKPA was modified by the Federal Defense of Marriage Act of 1996. DOMA seeks to "define and protect the institution of marriage" by establishing a federal definition of marriage as exclusively heterosexual[5] and by setting forth the following rule to govern state choice of law cases: "No state, territory, or possession of the United States, or Indian tribe, shall be required to give effect to any public act, record, or judicial proceeding of any other State, territory, possession, or tribe respecting a relationship between persons of the same sex that is treated as a marriage under the laws of such other State, territory, possession, or tribe, or a right or claim arising from such relationship."[6]

Lisa argued that the Vermont judgment that Janet had parental rights was a judgment "respecting a relationship between persons of the same sex that is treated as a marriage under the laws of" another state and thus was *not* entitled to full faith and credit. The Virginia court agreed with Lisa. As this is written, the case is being appealed.

If the Virginia court is correct, then no parental right arising out of a same-sex marriage is secure anywhere in the United States. The parents must always worry that the child could be kidnapped and taken to another state, where the non-biological parent would be unable to assert parental rights. And the nonbiological parent had better not travel with the child into Virginia, or the child might be taken away and put into foster care until some biological relative came to claim it.

This is not what Congress intended.

The Confused Origins of DOMA

DOMA was Congress's reaction to what seemed to be the imminent recognition of same-sex marriage in Hawaii (see Chapter 1). It passed both houses of Congress by huge margins.[7] Congress was afraid that, once same-sex marriages were recognized in Hawaii, other states would be required to recognize them, too.

DOMA is a silly and ill-conceived statute. It should be clear from earlier chapters that the fears that prompted Congress to act were based upon a massive misunderstanding of existing law. States have always had the power to decline to recognize marriages from other states, and they have been exercising that power for centuries.

The supporters of DOMA feared that recognition would be required by the full faith and credit clause of the Constitution, which reads: "Full Faith and Credit shall be given in each State to the public Acts, Records, and judicial Proceedings of every other State. And Congress may by General Laws prescribe the Manner in which such Acts, Records and Proceedings shall be proved, and the Effect thereof."[8] Congress thought that by invoking the last part of the provision, it could avoid the difficulty by prescribing that same-sex marriages need not have any effect.

The full faith and credit clause was drawn from similar language in the Articles of Confederation. There was little discussion of the provision in the Philadelphia constitutional convention. It's not clear whether it was originally intended only to provide that public records must be admitted into evidence, or whether it was to tell courts what weight to give them. Congress quickly adopted the latter interpretation, and since 1790 the rule has been that a judgment—a final decision of a court that ends a legal case—is to be given the same effect that it would have in the state that issued it.[9]

For some years now, the press has fecklessly repeated the claim that the full faith and credit clause will require every state to recognize same-sex marriages. Legal scholars have had to say, over and over, that this is a fundamental misconception.[10] The difficulty can be shown with a common sense illustration. Some states issue licenses to carry concealed handguns. Could full faith and credit possibly mean that the holders of such licenses have the right to carry concealed handguns anywhere in the United States? And, as it happens, there is not a single judicial decision that holds that full faith and credit requires states to recognize marriages that violate their own public policies concerning who may marry.[11] It has been suggested that Congress can legislate in response to ambiguity or uncertainty,[12] but there is no uncertainty here. Full faith and credit does not require other states to recognize same-sex marriages from Massachusetts.

What Full Faith and Credit Requires

Except for judgments of courts, the full faith and credit clause has never been much of a constraint on states' power to fashion choice of law rules. The Supreme Court has held that full faith and credit does not impose any limitation on a state's choice of law distinct from the limitation imposed by the requirements of due process.[13] The due process clauses of the Fifth and Fourteenth Amendments[14] have been understood to mean that any litigation must meet a test of fundamental fairness. Even if a case is properly before a court, that court could, in some circumstances, violate the parties' rights by applying its own law to the case. It might change the parties' rights in ways that they could never have anticipated. This would be unfair. The rule of law means, among other things, that people know in advance what rules are going to apply to their actions.

But unfair surprise won't happen in any case in which the parties could reasonably have anticipated that the court would apply its own law to them. This is why the full faith and credit clause does not require Illinois, for instance, to recognize the marriage of a same-sex couple who marry on a weekend trip to Cape Cod. It isn't unfair to apply Illinois law to people who live in Illinois. Illinois is the only state that will be affected by the continuing existence of their marriage. The couple has every reason to expect that Illinois's law will apply to their relationship. The constitutional test is fairness, and there is nothing unfair about applying the law of the state that has the greatest legitimate interest in the underlying transaction.

At this point, we need to distinguish choice of law from jurisdiction. Jurisdiction refers to a court's power to hear a case. Here the issue is not what state's law applies, but where a given case can be heard. It is sometimes reasonable for a court to exercise jurisdiction even if it has no good reason to apply its own law.

Suppose man A borrows money from man B in New York and then absconds with the money to Illinois. And further suppose that the law of debts is somehow relevantly different in the two states. If B follows A to Illinois and sues him there, it is eminently fair for the Illinois courts to hear the case. A is in Illinois and is subject to the power of its courts. If B can't sue A there, he may not be able to sue A anywhere. But at the time of the loan, the parties had no reason to think that the transaction would be governed by any state's law other than New York's. It would be unfair to apply Illinois law. So Illinois courts would have good reason to accept jurisdiction, but they would also have good reason to apply New York law.

The constitutional tests for jurisdiction and for choice of law sound similar, but they are distinct. In order to have jurisdiction over the parties, the forum must have "minimum contacts . . . such that the maintenance of the suit does not offend 'traditional notions of fair play and substantial justice.'"[15] It is remarkable how little contact will satisfy this test. A court once upheld a service of process (the summons to court that begins a lawsuit) on an airplane that was flying over (without ever landing in) the forum state.[16] Because the defendant had been physically present in Arkansas—albeit only for a short time, and thousands of feet above the ground—he could be forced to respond to a suit filed in an Arkansas court.

In order for a forum to be able to apply its own law, however, its contacts with the underlying transaction must be more than minimal. There must be "'a significant contact, or significant aggregation of contacts, creating state interests, such that [a state's] choice of its law is neither arbitrary nor fundamentally unfair.'"[17] Cases thus sometimes arise in which the court has jurisdiction to hear a case but no significant contact with the transaction. This means that sometimes, a state's courts will have the authority to hear a case but will not be permitted to use that state's law to decide the case. This is what the Supreme Court's two verbal formulas amount to: even very minimal contact with the state, such as the accident of being briefly present within a state's borders, is enough to get a person served with process and forced to appear in a state's courts. But that state can't apply its own law to that person unless it is fair to do so.

This constraint will rarely be relevant in litigation. Where it is not, DOMA won't be relevant, either.

What DOMA Actually Does

One must strain a bit to imagine situations in which the due process requirement would be relevant, but the exercise is worth undertaking because only by imagining such unusual (but possible) cases can one discern whatever effect the choice of law provision of DOMA has on existing law.

Consider, then, two hypothetical cases. I set both in Georgia, where mere transient presence is enough to give the courts jurisdiction,[18] and where there is a very sweeping mini-DOMA.[19]

> Anne, who lives and works in Massachusetts, is insured by a group health insurance plan that is paid for by Anne's employer. The insurance policy specifies that coverage will be provided to the "spouse" of the named insured. Anne's same-sex spouse, Betty, becomes seriously ill, requiring expensive treatment. The insurance company would prefer not to pay for the treatments, even though they are plainly required by the terms of the policy. While Betty is on an airplane flying over Georgia on its way to another state, a representative of the insurance company serves Betty with a summons to appear in a declaratory judgment action that the insurer has filed in a Georgia court. In its pleadings, the insurer claims that, since Georgia law declares same-sex marriages void and makes unenforceable any contractual rights arising out of such marriages, the court should apply Georgia law and declare that Anne and Betty were never validly married and that the insurer therefore has no contractual liability to Betty. (If the Georgia court agrees with the insurer's claim,[20] a Massachusetts court would have to give full faith and credit to its judgment, which, because

it does not "treat" the relationship between Anne and Betty "as a marriage under the laws of" Georgia, is unaffected by DOMA.)[21]

During Charles's marriage to David, during which they have both always lived in Massachusetts, Charles has prospered in his business, while David has cared for their children at home. Charles now wants to become single again but would prefer that David not receive any share of the property that Charles has accumulated during the marriage. While both are on an airplane flying over Georgia, Charles serves David with a summons to appear in a declaratory judgment action that Charles has filed in a Georgia court. And so forth.

In each of these cases, the application of Georgia law would violate due process. Georgia had no contact with the parties or the transaction before the filing of the suit. There is no legitimate reason for applying Georgia's substantive law to the case. Each case presents what proponents of the interest-analysis approach to conflict of laws call a "false conflict," because only one state has a legitimate interest in having its law applied.

The results that DOMA thus licenses are indefensible. There is no evidence that the proponents of DOMA wanted to defend them. The authors of the law do not appear to have given any thought to these possibilities. Both of these are unusual cases, but it is only in such unusual cases that DOMA's choice of law provision can have any effect on preexisting law.

This issue of fundamental fairness hardly ever arises in choice of law litigation. Where it does, however, Congress cannot make it go away. Due process is as much of a constraint on Congress as it is on the states. Even if Congress has plenary authority over the scope of full faith and credit,[22] it cannot exercise that authority in ways that violate the rights of individuals. When states devise choice of law rules, therefore, the only constraint imposed upon them by the Constitution is one that Congress cannot remove. DOMA, then, can have no effect on the states' freedom to craft choice of law rules dealing with the recognition of marriage.

There is, however, one way in which DOMA plainly alters preexisting law. The Supreme Court has enforced the full faith and credit clause only weakly with respect to laws, but it has enforced it quite strictly with respect to judgments. It has been settled for nearly a century that no state may refuse to enforce a final judgment issued by the courts of another state.[23] The basic idea is that litigation has to come to an end. The losing party can't be allowed to just go to another court and try to reopen the matter. It would be unfair to the parties, and it would also make courts look ridiculous if they constantly contradicted each other.[24] This is why divorces are entitled to full faith and credit, and why Nevada was therefore able, for a long time, to set itself up as a divorce haven for residents of states where divorces were hard to get: a divorce is an adversarial proceeding between the spouses, and the divorce decree is a judicial judgment, no less than an award of money in a suit for a debt. And all judgments are final. At some point, litigation has to come to an end.

Here is where DOMA has a radical, and strange, effect. DOMA's provision that a state need not even give effect to a "judicial proceeding" respecting a same-sex marriage implies that *all* judgments in which the prevailing party pleaded the existence of a same-sex marriage can be ignored by other states.

If a drunk driver kills a pedestrian on a Boston street, the victim happens to have been married to a person of the same sex, and the surviving spouse wins a wrongful death suit, could the driver avoid the consequences by fleeing with his money to a state that does not recognize same-sex marriage? DOMA's plain language says he could.

To make matters more complicated, federal law, as amended by DOMA, withdraws full faith and credit only from judgments in which the rendering court *recognizes* a same-sex marriage, while continuing to require full faith and credit for judgments in which the rendering court *denies* recognition. Only the former is a "judicial proceeding of any other State . . . respecting a relationship between persons of the same sex that is treated as a marriage under the laws of such other State." Thus, a court's decision will or will not be entitled to full faith and credit, depending on whether it reaches a result that Congress likes.

This invites scenarios that are *really* weird. In the wrongful death case just discussed, if the drunk driver filed a counterclaim for a declaratory judgment and relitigated the liability question in the new forum, and the court held that no wrongful death suit could proceed because no marriage ever existed, *that* judgment would be entitled to full faith and credit everywhere—*even in Massachusetts.* The defendant would then be free to return home to Boston and put his money back in the bank there, secure in the knowledge that federal law would protect his assets from seizure by his victim's survivors.

If, on the other hand, the new forum state refused to collude in this evasion and reconfirmed the Massachusetts judgment, this second judgment, too, would under DOMA be disentitled to full faith and credit because this second judgment, too, would have recognized the existence of a same-sex marriage. The defendant would then be free to relitigate the question anew in a third forum, and a fourth, and so on. Whenever at last he found a court that would cooperate with his scheme, the judgment issued by *that* forum would then be entitled to full faith and credit throughout the United States!

The odd result in the Miller-Jenkins case follows a similar logic. The open legal question there is whether DOMA partially repeals PKPA. PKPA was necessary because the 1790 statute provides that judgments should be given the same effect that they are given in the state that hands them down. In most cases, courts treat judgments as final; the merits of a case cannot be revisited later. Any child custody judgment, however, can be reconsidered by the court in light of changed circumstances. A court that gives a mother custody will always want to reconsider that decision if she becomes abusive, for example. The rule that custody orders are never final meant that, if a court in state B, to which a child had been abducted, reopened the judgment of state A, it was not violating the 1790 statute. The state B court would not have done anything that a state A court could not have done. This loophole was an incentive for disgruntled parents to defy custody judgments by kidnapping their children. PKPA was passed in order to close that loophole.

DOMA provides that a state need not "give effect to any . . . judicial proceeding of any other State . . . respecting a relationship between persons of the same sex that is treated as a marriage under the laws of such other State . . . or a right or claim arising from such relationship." Since a claim like Janet's is a claim arising from such a relationship, so the argument would go, it is covered by DOMA, and PKPA's requirement to the contrary is to that extent repealed. If this is so, then children of same-sex couples are denied the protection of PKPA.

These are bizarre results, but they are the only way in which the choice of law provision of DOMA changes the status quo. As I will explain shortly, such results probably mean that DOMA is unconstitutional.

In writing the provision to cover judgments as well as choice of law decisions, Congress does not seem to have contemplated any genuinely adversarial proceeding, even though this is the only kind of proceeding that can generate a judgment entitled to full faith and credit. Some gay rights advocates had suggested that a couple traveling to Hawaii to marry should also get a declaratory judgment of the marriage's validity.[25] The House committee report, citing these writers, noted that "it is possible that homosexual couples could obtain a judicial judgment memorializing their 'marriage,' and then proceed to base their claim of sister-state recognition on that judicial record."[26] The report therefore states plainly that DOMA applies to "judicial orders."[27] Again, Congress conjured up a bogey without substance. In a forum with a strong public policy against recognizing same-sex marriage, a court would certainly hold that the domicile state is not bound by a collusive judgment to which it was not a party.[28]

DOMA's Unconstitutionality

DOMA is likely unconstitutional. Recall, from Chapter 5, the equal protection problems that are created by a blanket rule of nonrecognition. DOMA licenses precisely that rule. Our discussion concluded that *Romer v. Evans*[29] and *Lawrence v. Texas*[30] together establish a fairly clear rule: *If a law singles out gays for unprecedentedly harsh treatment, the court will presume that what is going on is a bare desire to harm, rather than mere moral disapproval.* In both cases, the statute in question singled out gays for extraordinary burdens. That is what DOMA does, too. Every single way in which it changes existing law is unprecedented and is so bizarre as to be indefensible.

Some scholars have suggested one way to rehabilitate DOMA: simply hold it to be declaratory of existing law. It was, in effect, the equivalent of a congressional declaration that the sky is blue. Its sole purpose and effect was to dispel the misunderstandings that had been in circulation.[31]

Such a construction would forestall all the odd effects we have discussed. It is consistent with an understanding of the environment in which DOMA was passed, in which the press ignorantly repeated lurid claims that full faith and credit law would automatically obligate every state to recognize same-sex marriages for all purposes. Congress, on this account, performed a useful function by restating, in the most prominent possible way, what already was the law: that for many purposes, states have no obligation to recognize marriages that are contrary to their public policies.[32] This is an excessively charitable construction of DOMA, but excessively charitable constructions are part of the business of courts when it is necessary to save a statute from unconstitutionality.[33]

This is probably closer to Congress's intent than the literal interpretations we have just been considering, which produce crazy results. And it is consistent with some familiar rules for interpreting statutes. Inconsistencies among statutes are not generally interpreted to imply that the earlier statute is repealed, wholly or in part.[34] Yet this is what we must say if DOMA is to partly repeal PKPA because PKPA is not mentioned in DOMA or even in the House committee report accompanying DOMA. Another conventional rule is that statutes should not be read literally when this would produce absurd results.[35] William Blackstone wrote long ago that "where some collateral matter arises out of the general words, and happens to be unreasonable; there the judges are in decency to conclude that this consequence was not foreseen."[36]

But there is another canon of statutory construction that cuts the other way. Laws should not be construed in such a way that they have no effect whatsoever on preexisting law. On the contrary, every word of a statute is to be construed so that it has some effect.[37] DOMA's choice of law provision is poorly drafted, but its language is too plain (and, with respect to judgments, too clearly supported by the legislative history) to be construed away. This plain language, we have seen, produces results that cannot be rationally related to any permissible state purpose. The only end to which this provision has any rational relation is the bare desire to harm same-sex couples—to authorize state courts to ignore sister state judgments if and only if those judgments vindicate the marital interests of such couples. Since the only effects that DOMA can possibly have are unconstitutional ones, perhaps it is not possible to save the law from invalidation.

President George W. Bush used this possibility as a justification for a constitutional amendment barring same-sex marriage: "there is no assurance that the Defense of Marriage Act will not, itself, be struck down by activist courts. In that event, every state would be forced to recognize any relationship that judges in Boston or officials in San Francisco choose to call a marriage."[38]

The president is, to put it most charitably, confused. Even if DOMA is struck down, this would merely mean that same-sex marriages could not be disregarded in the extraordinary cases we have just considered. In the routine marriage evasion case in which an Illinois couple marries during a weekend trip to Boston and immediately returns to Chicago, Illinois courts would not be required to recognize the marriage. DOMA's constitutionality is nearly irrelevant to choice of law because DOMA has so little effect on preexisting choice of law rules.

The Unconstitutionality of DOMA's Definitional Provision

There is, however, another part of DOMA that radically changes preexisting law. And because of this part, the unconstitutionality of DOMA matters quite a lot.

Although, when the bill was being debated, most of the press's attention focused on the choice of law provision of DOMA, sometimes implying that it was the only substantive provision of the bill, the definitional provision was far more important. It provides the following: "In determining the meaning of any Act of Congress, or of any ruling, regulation, or interpretation of the various administrative bureaus and agencies of the United States, the word 'marriage' means only a legal union between one man and one woman as husband and wife and the word 'spouse' refers only to a person of the opposite sex who is a husband or wife."[39]

Given the broad range of federal laws to which marital status is relevant, the consequences of this definitional provision are far-reaching:

- Same-sex spouses cannot file joint tax returns.
- Same-sex spouses' debts incurred under divorce decrees or separation agreements are dischargeable in bankruptcy.[40]
- Same-sex spouses of federal employees are excluded from the Federal Employees Health Benefits Program,[41] the Federal Employees Group

Life Insurance Program,[42] and the Federal Employees Compensation Act, which compensates the widow or widower of an employee killed in the performance of duty.[43]

- Same-sex spouses are the only surviving widows and widowers who do not have automatic ownership rights in a copyrighted work after the author's death.[44]

- Same-sex spouses lack federal protection against enforcement of due-on-sale clauses, which allow a lender to declare the entire balance due and payable if mortgaged property is transferred, and which could compel the loss of the family home if the holder of the mortgage dies and the spouse inherits the property.[45]

- Same-sex spouses are denied the benefit of the Family and Medical Leave Act of 1993, which provides for up to twelve weeks per year of unpaid leave to employees for, among other purposes, "care for a spouse."[46]

- Same-sex spouses are similarly unable to receive benefits under the Social Security Act's Old Age, Survivors, and Disability Insurance Program.[47]

- Same-sex spouses are denied preferential treatment under immigration law and are, therefore, the only legally married spouses of American citizens who face deportation.[48]

This second provision of DOMA may be unwise, inhumane, and insulting, but its constitutionality seems, on first blush, to be secure from doubt. Congress obviously has the power to define the terms of the U.S. Code. The only way to challenge this provision is to claim that it is impermissibly discriminatory.[49] All discrimination claims allege the abuse of a power that the actor concededly possesses. Congress could not define "marriage" to mean only a legal union between people of the same race.[50] But the constitutional significance of discrimination against *gay people* is uncertain. The federal courts have been unwilling to hold that laws that target gays are always constitutionally suspect, and the Supreme Court has not directly confronted the question. But, as we have already seen, *Lawrence* and *Romer* show that there are limits on what the state may do to gay people.

DOMA's definitional provision and the amendment invalidated in *Romer* have telling similarities. Like the Colorado amendment, this provision "identifies persons by a single trait [membership in a same-sex marriage] and then denies them protection across the board."[51] Congress does not seem to have given any specific consideration to the broad range of federal policies to which spousal status is relevant, or to have made any effort to justify the numerous specific disabilities that the statute imposed.[52] For the first time in American history, DOMA creates a set of second-class marriages, which are valid under state law but void for all federal purposes. The exclusion of a class of valid state marriages from all federal recognition is "unprecedented in our jurisprudence."[53] DOMA's "general announcement that [the lawful civil marriages of] gays and lesbians shall not have any particular protections from the law,"[54] its critics have argued, demonstrates its lack of any legitimate purpose and compels the inference that, like Amendment 2, it rests on a bare desire to harm a politically unpopular group.

A defender of the statute could reply, however, that the disability it imposes, though broad, is proportionate to the situation that called it forth. DOMA's definitions of "marriage" and "spouse," the House committee report observed, merely restate "the current understanding of what those terms mean for purposes of federal law."[55] When Congress used the term "marriage" in the U.S. Code, it never imagined that this term would include same-sex couples.[56] Hawaii's adoption of same-sex marriage "would radically alter a basic premise upon which the presumption of adoption [for federal purposes] of state domestic relations law was based—namely, the essential fungibility of the concepts of 'marriage' from one state to another."[57] This provision of DOMA, then, "merely reaffirm[s] what is already known, what is already in place."[58] It is hard to see how a law that simply declares the status quo can be unconstitutionally discriminatory.

The *Romer* analogy doesn't devastate DOMA because there are significant disanalogies as well. Unlike Amendment 2, the definitional provision does not "outrun and belie any legitimate justifications that may be claimed for it."[59] Amendment 2's license to discriminate against gays was so broadly worded that it seemed to the Court likely to mandate some unconstitutional applications. This fact bespoke a bare desire to harm gays. There is, on the other hand, no fundamental right to file a joint tax return or to receive social security benefits. The discrimination against same-sex couples may be unprecedented, a defender of DOMA could say, but so is the situation that called the law forth. If there is any positive value to the tradition of restricting marriage to one man and one woman, then this positive value provides a rational basis for DOMA. One cannot confidently infer, simply by considering the definitional provision on its face, that its purpose is a desire to harm the group. That *might* be the purpose, but an innocent explanation is available. The Court has often been prone to credit innocent explanations of statutes, even those that harm constitutionally protected groups.[60] In order for the law to be invalidated, there has to be some reason to disbelieve that explanation.

The statute's targeting of gays and the uniqueness of the disability imposed provide some of the needed evidence of invidious purpose. "[L]aws singling out a certain class of citizens for disfavored legal status are rare,"[61] and "'[d]iscriminations of an unusual character especially suggest careful consideration to determine whether they are obnoxious to the constitutional provision.'"[62] But where is this "careful consideration" to lead? *Romer* relied—how heavily?—on the fact that no innocent explanation of the statute seemed even facially plausible. The Court's opinion does not indicate what should be done if the state is able to proffer such an innocent explanation. An equal protection challenge to the definitional provision of DOMA, standing alone, would be a hard case.

This difficulty is resolved, however, if we read the rest of the statute.

When one mounts a similar attack on the choice of law provision, these difficulties vanish.[63] The choice of law provision of DOMA, like the definitional provision, "identifies persons by a single trait [membership in a same-sex marriage] and then denies them protection across the board."[64] But it is hard to explain *this* provision's breadth in terms of the narrow situation it seeks to address. The choice of law provision goes well beyond anything necessary to ensure "that each State can define for itself the concept of marriage and not be bound by decisions made by other States."[65] It permits states to disregard the marriages of same-sex couples under any circumstances, even when the forum state has so little contact with the couples that it would be unconstitutional for it to apply its own marriage law to them. The *Romer* Court thought it relevant that the Colorado amendment's "disqualification of a class of persons from the right to seek specific protection from the law [was] unprecedented in our jurisprudence."[66] Similarly, no group whose marriages were prohibited by some states—not married first cousins, not members of polygamous marriages, not even interracial couples, whose marriages were punishable as felonies in the Jim Crow states—has ever had its marriages, validly recognized in one jurisdiction, subjected to the degree of ostracism by others that DOMA licenses.

Unlike the definitional section, the choice of law section's operation cannot plausibly be described as a measured response to the situation that called it forth. As we have seen, the results it authorizes are ones no one could have intended. Its broad sweep divorces it "from any factual context from which we could discern a relationship to legitimate state interests."[67] Like Amendment 2, the effects of the choice of law provision "outrun and belie any legitimate justifications that may be claimed for it."[68] Like Amendment 2, "its sheer breadth is so discontinuous with the reasons offered for it that the [law] seems inexplicable by anything but animus toward the class that it affects."[69]

What does this imply about the other provision of DOMA, which merely defines marriage?

Michael Dorf observes that if a statute has an "impermissible purpose, courts cannot save it by severing its unconstitutional applications. The invalid legislative purpose pervades all of the provision's applications."[70] The constitutional defects of DOMA's choice of law provision put its definitional provision in a different light. The bill's proponents argued that the definitional section merely preserves the status quo, but that section accomplishes its end by doing something unprecedented.

Same-sex marriages are assigned a legal pariah status that has never before existed in American history. Of all the married couples in the country, only the marriages of same-sex couples will not be recognized by the federal government—ever, for any purpose, no matter how much they may resemble, for relevant purposes, all other married couples. (If two federal employees are killed in the line of duty, is the same-sex spouse of one less deserving of compensation than the opposite-sex spouse of the other?)[71] If impermissible animus pervades the choice of law provision of DOMA, the same animus infects the definitional section, in which the federal government "deem[s] a class of persons a stranger to its laws."[72] In the context of the bill as a whole, the innocent explanation of the definitional provision loses credibility.

Ordinarily, Dorf observes, "if the purpose of one provision of a statute is invalid, but other provisions serve valid legislative purposes, then the invalid portion may be severed subject only to conventional severability constraints."[73] Conventional severability principles would certainly call for preserving the definitional provision of DOMA, even if the choice of law provision were invalidated.[74] However, as we saw earlier, there is already some doubt as to whether the definitional provision itself serves valid legislative purposes. It is no accident that the two provisions of DOMA happen to be in the same bill. This was not an omnibus budget reconciliation act. If there is no way to escape the inference that the purpose of DOMA's choice of law provision was to harm the affected group, then this inference ought to extend to the definitional provision, which targets the same group and injures it even more severely than the choice of law provision does.[75]

DOMA is unconstitutional because of its invidious purpose. I possess no knowledge of, and am making no claim about, any legislator's or staff member's subjective state of mind. Members of Congress may be guilty of nothing worse than sloppy draftsmanship. But the purpose of DOMA that appears plainly on its face, the only end to which the statute is suited, is a bare desire to harm a politically unpopular group. This purpose is unconstitutional.

So the definitional provision, which is by far the most important part of DOMA, is invalid because it is part of the same statutory scheme as the invalid choice of law provision. One contaminates the other. Of course, Congress could get around this difficulty by repassing the definitional provision as a freestanding statute. It is uncertain, however, whether the definitional provision alone would get enough support to pass. One recent poll shows that 55 percent think that gay partners should receive Social Security benefits. Only 36 percent think they should not.[76] Perhaps the only reason why DOMA passed so easily is because the public was befuddled about what was really at stake.

Finally, DOMA should have no effect whatsoever upon state courts' deliberations on the recognition of same-sex marriages in any individual choice of law case. The public may have been confused about the applicable choice of law principles. Sitting judges presumably were not, and did not need instruction from Congress about the applicable law.

IX

The Difference the
Mini-DOMAs Make

Although the federal Defense of Marriage Act is irrelevant to the question of when and whether same-sex marriages will be recognized, the numerous *state* statutes declaring a strong public policy against same-sex marriage, or mini-DOMAs, are much more pertinent. I have deferred discussion of these laws until now because statutes operate against a background of preexisting law. We had to be clear on what that preexisting law was before we could explore the mini-DOMAs and their effects.

These statutes were enacted in three waves in response to the progress of the movement toward same-sex marriage described in Chapter 1. In the early 1970s, reacting to a few lawsuits filed by same-sex couples who sought to marry, a number of states enacted laws declaring that marriage would only be recognized between a man and a woman. A larger wave of statutes was enacted after the 1993 Hawaii Supreme Court decision that made it seem likely that that state would shortly recognize same-sex marriage. Finally, the most recent wave of laws and constitutional amendments followed the decisions in which state supreme courts in Vermont and Massachusetts construed their states' constitutions as mandating recognition of same-sex relationships.

As this is written in October 2005, forty states have post-1993 mini-DOMAs: Alabama, Alaska, Arizona, Arkansas, California, Colorado, Delaware, Florida, Georgia, Hawaii, Idaho, Illinois, Indiana, Iowa, Kansas, Kentucky, Louisiana, Maine, Michigan, Minnesota, Mississippi, Missouri, Montana, Nebraska, Nevada, North Carolina, North Dakota, Ohio, Oklahoma, Oregon, Pennsylvania, South Carolina, South Dakota, Tennessee, Texas, Utah, Vermont, Virginia, Washington, and West Virginia. (The mini-DOMAs in California and Vermont have not stopped those states from recognizing domestic partnerships and civil unions because those statuses do not use the name "marriage.") Three states have pre-1993 statutes barring same-sex marriage: Maryland (1973), New Hampshire (1987), and Wyoming (1977). (Many other states had pre-1993 statutes but reworded them after the Hawaii decision to address the interstate recognition issue.) Connecticut does not directly address the issue, but its adoption law declares that the state's public policy limits marriage to a man and a woman.[1] Same-sex marriages are recognized, and licenses continue to be issued, in Massachusetts. There is no authority on the question in five states: New Jersey, New Mexico, New York, Rhode Island, and Wisconsin.

Each wave of statutes was enacted in response to a specific problem that seemed likely to materialize:

> 1. An application for a marriage license by same-sex couples, who might argue that there was

nothing in the statutes restricting marriage to opposite-sex couples.

2. An evasive foreign marriage by residents of the state, who would immediately return home and demand that their marriage be recognized.

3. A decision by the state supreme court mandating recognition of same-sex relationships.

Most of the mini-DOMAs efficiently eliminate the threat that provoked them. Oddly, though, some of them are so clumsily worded that they don't even clearly reach the evasion case. There are, however, other scenarios that are sure to materialize sooner or later and that evidently got no attention at all.

4. People migrating to the state.

5. People temporarily passing through the state.

6. Marriages of people who never set foot in the state as a married couple but whose status is relevant to litigation in the state.

7. Children of same-sex couples who enter the state, temporarily or permanently, and whose status may need to be determined.

8. Individual same-sex spouses entering the state who seek to avoid obligations of marital property and child support.

9. People entering the state trying to avoid money judgments rendered after trial in another state.

10. Same-sex spouses entering the state who seek declarations of nullity from the state's courts.

11. People entering the state who wish to contract new marriages without having to dissolve, or perhaps even to disclose, previous ones.

Some of the new statutes are so broadly worded that they reach all of these cases.

Most of the statutes do not necessarily go any farther than the evasion cases, which as we have seen are the strongest cases for nonrecognition. If a state has a right to ban same-sex marriage, then it can reasonably refuse to recognize such marriages by its residents who fly to Boston for a day to get married. This is the type of case that almost all of these laws were intended to address. Some of these laws' provisions state that marriage licenses may not be issued to people of the same sex, which says nothing about the effect of marriages celebrated elsewhere.[2] Statements that such marriages are "void" or "prohibited" or both[3] are ambiguous and do not clearly reach extraterritorial marriages.[4] Some specify that such marriages are invalid within the jurisdiction, which leaves open the status of couples living outside the state.[5] Others deem them contrary to the state's public policy, but it is not made clear whether that public policy is so strong that the state will attempt to apply it to transactions, in or out of the state, involving nondomiciliaries.[6]

Even the strongest public policy language used in these laws is constrained by history. It is a commonplace rule of statutory interpretation that when terminology has previously appeared in earlier statutes, and has been interpreted by courts to have a certain meaning, it should be understood to mean the same thing in a new statute.[7] The language used by these mini-DOMAs was ubiquitous in the miscegenation statutes, which usually declared interracial marriages "void" and "prohibited."[8] The cases described in Chapter 3 all involved statutes using one or more of these terms, and the southern courts usually recognized nonevasive interracial marriages.[9] If such language did not bar recognition in those cases, it should not do so now, either. In this context, "void" evidently means "void for residents of this state," not "void for anyone in the world whose marriage is in any way pertinent to litigation in our courts."[10]

Maine's statute declares that "[p]ersons of the same sex may not contract marriage" and further provides that such marriages are "considered void if the parties take up residence in this State."[11] This appears to mean that nonrecognition is the rule in migratory cases but not in visitor cases. This draws the lines more intelligently than blanket nonrecognition, but it is nonetheless cruder than its authors probably intended. Does Maine really mean to say that a same-sex marriage in nearby Massachusetts is no impediment to a subsequent marriage in Maine by someone who permanently takes up residence in Maine? Or that a person moving to Maine could be thereby relieved of spousal property claims and child support obligations?

Most of these laws apply only to same-sex *marriages* from other states, but those of Arkansas, Georgia, Kentucky, Louisiana, Michigan, Nebraska, North Dakota, Ohio, Texas, Utah, and Virginia also bar recognition of same-sex relationships that resemble marriage, evidently meaning statuses such as California domestic partnerships and Connecticut and Vermont civil unions. These statutes also generally do not make clear whether they apply to any but evasive unions.[12] As usual, the more complex conflicts scenarios were never thought of.

Some of the statutes, particularly the most recent ones, are so broad that they approach blanket nonrecognition. These harsher statutes can be grouped into three categories. The first category focuses, oddly, on refusing to enforce any "contractual rights" created by same-sex marriages. The meaning of these laws is obscure. The second category declares that the state will not enforce judgments of other states' courts if those judgments are based on recognition of same-sex marriages. And the third category imposes a broad blanket rule of nonrecognition. Laws in these last two categories are probably unconstitutional because they impose broad and sweeping disabilities on a single group: same-sex couples.

Contractual Rights

Statutes in Alaska, Arkansas, Minnesota, and Virginia focus on denying "contractual rights" arising out of same-sex marriage. Here, for example, is the language of the Alaska statute, the first of these laws to be enacted, which the other statutes evidently have emulated: "A marriage entered into by persons of the same sex, either under common law or under statute, that is recognized by another state or foreign jurisdiction is void in this state, and contractual rights granted by virtue of the marriage, including its termination, are unenforceable in this state."[13] Nearly identical language appears in the laws of Minnesota and Virginia.[14]

The clause referring to "contractual rights" makes little sense. Rights that arise by virtue of a marriage, such as rights of intestate succession or hospital visitation, are not contractual rights. (Minnesota's statute declares that marriage "is a civil contract between a man and a woman," but this is a metaphor, not a statement of the law.) They arise not out of a contract, but by operation of law. It makes even less sense to refer to contractual rights granted by virtue of the termination of a marriage. Rights that arise out of a marriage's termination are the consequence of a court's orders, not a contract. The language rests on a category mistake. It is like referring to marriage rights that are blue or that are in the key of B flat.[15]

Under the most plausible interpretation of this language, it precludes the approach, suggested in Chapter 7, of construing marital rights as contract rights. I suggested there that, in states that do not allow same-sex marriage, the marriages of couples who migrate to the state should be treated as though they were ordinary contracts and given the same legal effect as the marital rights that the parties could have expressly created by contract. This would spare the parties the expensive task of drawing up legal documents that would confer those rights. This solution now seems to be unavailable in Alaska, Arkansas, Minnesota, and Virginia.[16] It is precluded by the plain language of these statutes, although it is doubtful that any of the drafters had this tactic in mind. Any married same-sex couple migrating to those states would be well advised to try to replicate their marital rights by contract. Any rights that arise from that contract will not be granted by virtue of the marriage license, and so will be enforceable.

Another possible reading is that the reference to contract is sloppy surplusage, and that these statutes mandate a blanket rule of nonrecognition. In this case, these laws would be unconstitutional for all the reasons reviewed in Chapter 5.

Three states, Virginia, Montana, and Michigan, go even farther and apparently bar same-sex couples from even conferring marriage-like rights upon one another by contract.[17] These laws are almost certainly unconstitutional.

Virginia has two statutes that refer to "contractual rights." One of them, already cited, adopts the confused formulation of Alaska. The other—adopted later, over the governor's veto—is clearer but astonishingly broad: "A civil union, partnership contract or other arrangement between persons of the same sex purporting to bestow the privileges or obligations of marriage is prohibited. Any such civil union, partnership contract or other arrangement entered into by persons of the same sex in another state or jurisdiction shall be void in all respects in Virginia and any contractual rights created thereby shall be void and unenforceable."[18]

This provision is so broad that it appears to bar enforcement of any "arrangement," which apparently means any legal document of any kind, between members of a same-sex couple that gives them any of the rights that the law gives to a married couple. A will, a medical power of attorney, a deed transferring an interest in a piece of real estate, even a form authorizing another to pick up a child from school, would all be void to the extent that it tries to create any right that exists by law between the members of a married couple.

The governor worried about "the right of people to enter into legal relationships," but the legislation was enacted without amendment. The consequence is that some same-sex couples have begun to leave Virginia, fearful that all the legal documents they have relied on for years will now be unenforceable. One Fredericksburg couple felt pressured to move away after living there for forty years. The state attorney general, defending the law's constitutionality, denied that the law would have this effect: "The purpose of this legislation is not to prohibit business partnership agreements, medical directives, joint bank accounts, or any other rights or privileges not exclusive to the institution of marriage."[19] But what he is offering is a very bold, narrowing construction of the law, one that makes its reach less sweeping than its plain language indicates.

A similar statute in Montana is only slightly narrower, prohibiting "a marriage between persons of the same sex" and declaring that a "contractual relationship entered into for the purpose of achieving a civil relationship that is prohibited . . . is void as against public policy."[20] This reaches only contracts, not other arrangements, between same-sex couples, but it still makes them void. Like Virginia's law, it declares that members of same-sex couples are forbidden to do what everyone else is permitted to do.

Michigan's constitutional amendment similarly provides that "the union of one man and one woman in marriage shall be the only agreement recognized as a marriage or similar union for any purpose."[21] The last six words of this provision are so broad that they would arguably preclude any two adults, including but not limited to a same-sex couple, from trying to make an agreement that is "similar . . . for any purpose" to a marriage. The meaning of this one is *really* obscure. It's not clear how similar to a marriage an agreement has to be in order to be prohibited—probably the law doesn't bar ordinary business partnerships—but the most natural reading, in context, is that it precludes contracts entered into by same-sex couples, and only by those couples, which confer rights that married couples would be entitled to.

These laws are almost certainly unconstitutional. Recall *Romer v. Evans,*[22] discussed in Chapter 5, in which the Supreme Court invalidated a law that had "the peculiar property of imposing a broad and undifferentiated disability on a single named group."[23] That law, the Court observed, would apparently "deprive[] gays and lesbians even of the protection of general laws and policies that prohibit arbitrary discrimination in governmental and private settings."[24] Similarly here, same-sex couples are prohibited from making contracts that everyone else is allowed to make. As in *Romer,* each of these laws "classifies homosexuals not to further a proper legislative end but to make them unequal to everyone else."[25] It is not constitutionally permissible to say that gay people are denied legal protections that are available to all other citizens; "[a] State cannot so deem a class of persons a stranger to its laws."[26]

Nonenforcement of Judgments

A second category of statute indicates that judgments of courts will not be enforced if a same-sex marriage was at issue in the underlying lawsuit. Florida, Georgia, Ohio, Texas, and West Virginia indicate that they will not even recognize "judicial proceedings" arising from same-sex marriage.[27] For all the reasons canvassed in Chapter 8, this is unconstitutional. States have to enforce foreign judgments, whether or not they agree with what the court did in the other state. This *is* the minimum content of full faith and credit. State courts have an obligation to respect each other's decisions. Recall the bizarre results of a different rule: a drunk driver who kills a pedestrian in Boston, and who has been successfully sued for wrongful death by his victim's same-sex spouse, could avoid responsibility by fleeing with his money to Florida or Texas. The authors of these laws are unlikely to have aimed for this result. It is likely that they copied from the language of the federal DOMA. As we saw in Chapter 8, the reference to "judicial proceedings" made no sense in that context, and it is similarly nonsensical in this one. Like the bars on contracts by same-sex couples, these provisions hurt gay couples in such a broad and undifferentiated way that they, too, are unconstitutional.

Blanket Nonrecognition

Finally, six laws plainly adopt blanket nonrecognition.[28] For reasons already reviewed in Chapter 5, these are unconstitutional.

Two of these are especially egregious. One is that of Louisiana, the only state in which the legislature appears to have even thought about the choice of law issue outside the evasion scenario. Louisiana's Civil Code has a choice of law provision, which provides that "[t]he status of a natural person and the incidents and effects of that status are governed by the law of the state whose policies would be most seriously impaired if its law were not applied to the particular issue." That state is determined by considering, inter alia, "the relationship of each state, at any pertinent time, to the dispute, the parties, and the person whose status is at issue," and "the policies of sustaining the validity of obligations voluntarily undertaken, of protecting children, minors, and others in need of protection, and of preserving family values and stability."[29] Public policy can invalidate a marriage, but only if it is the public policy of the most interested state.[30] This is just a summary of one version of the most sophisticated contemporary choice of law theory.

Louisiana very recently had an entirely sensible choice of law regime in place. Under it, evasive marriages would rarely have been recognized, while a more complex analysis would be required for other cases. The state has now deliberately scrapped this nuanced approach in favor of a blanket rule of nonrecognition, which applies in this and no other context.[31] Once more, this is unconstitutional because it singles out same-sex couples for disabilities that are imposed on no one else. Everyone on the planet gets the benefit of Louisiana's ordinary choice of rule, except same-sex couples. They alone are subject to the blanket nonrecognition rule. Their marital and child support obligations are unenforceable in Louisiana courts. They alone may be unable to get their children back if those children are kidnapped and taken into Louisiana. And so forth. As argued at length in Chapter 5, a blanket nonrecognition rule is unconstitutional.

Texas recently amended its constitution to provide that the state and its subdivisions "may not create or recognize any legal status identical or similar to marriage."[32] This evidently was intended to forestall recognition of civil unions or domestic partnerships, but the provision is so clumsily drafted that, taken literally, it abolishes all marriages in Texas. Standard model heterosexual marriage is, of course, a "legal status identical or similar to marriage." Did Texas conclude that it had to destroy marriage in order to save it? Obviously, this wasn't the intention. The Texas example should make us cautious about interpreting these laws literally.

These overbroad laws are particularly ill considered because their unconstitutionality means that they cannot be given effect even to do what the state would clearly be permitted to do, such as ban evasive same-sex marriages. As argued in Chapter 8, the unconstitutionality of the federal DOMA infects the entire statute, including the otherwise permissible definitional section. The same contamination occurs at the state level. The unconstitutionality of these state statutes means that they are void in their entirety, unlike other, more moderate statutes that pursue the same end.

Let me be clear about what I am *not* saying. I am not claiming that the Constitution requires states to adopt all of the specific conflicts rules that I endorsed in Chapter 7. I already noted that a state can have a strong public policy against same-sex marriage. It can decline to recognize evasive marriages. It can permissibly decline to treat a same-sex marriage as a contract. It also need not give travelers the right to exercise marital rights, such as the right to file a wrongful death suit. There is room for argument about the details of a conflicts regime in this area. What states may not do is what too many of them have done: flail wildly at the problem, like a man in a crowded room singlemindedly trying to kill a mosquito with a baseball bat.

X
Toward Benign Competition

The status of same-sex couples who live in Massachusetts, Vermont, Connecticut, and California, states that give their relationships all the rights of married couples, is doubtful today whenever they leave their home state. These couples can (if they can afford good legal advice!) try to use legal instruments, such as wills, contracts, and powers of attorney, to duplicate their marital rights in order to make those rights portable to other states. But such stratagems cannot duplicate all the rights of marriage. As E. J. Graff writes about her own same-sex partnership, "the documents that Madeline and I have signed allow me to care for her if she's in a coma—but so long as she's conscious, no nurse or physician has any obligation to tell me anything about her condition or care." And even the protections they do afford are imperfectly reliable: "If we got hit by a Range Rover while vacationing in, say, Utah's Canyonlands or Wales—and we'd forgotten to pack our envelope of notarized papers (or if they'd burned when the car exploded)—how could I persuade the hospital that she belongs to me? I wouldn't even be able to lie and say we were married, as unmarried different-sex couples can. Every administrator, nurse, or physician could decide for themselves—based on their own ideologies—whether I had the right to know whether she was in the ICU, or surgery, or alive, or whether I could stay in her room overnight."[1]

The key question that remains unresolved today is the scope of the state mini-DOMAs. The most charitable interpretation of them is that they are defensive and seek only to prevent those states from having to recognize continuing same-sex marriages within their borders. Their authors were worried primarily about the evasion case and generally gave no thought to other cases. They wanted their own states' laws to maintain the normative position that heterosexual marriages have a value that same-sex marriages cannot possibly share.

But if the situation is one of self-defense, then some rules from the law of self-defense are relevant here. In criminal law, if you are attacked, you have a right to defend yourself. But your defense needs to be necessary and proportional to the scale of the attack.[2] No matter how badly your attacker behaved, your self-defense plea won't fly if he or she has been shot more than once, especially if some of the wounds are in the back.[3]

Some of the antigay laws that are now being passed go far beyond the protection of an ideal of marriage. They inflict serious harm in order to make a purely symbolic point. For instance, Florida expresses its disapproval of homosexual conduct with a statute that forbids gays from adopting children. Defenders of the statute claim that they believe children are best raised by parents of different sexes, but they ignore the actual consequence of the law, which is that large numbers of gay foster parents are barred from adopting the children who have grown up in their households.[4] Such children are in fact dependent on the relationships that the law refuses to recognize. Whatever this law is concerned with, it is not the welfare of these children.

As we saw in Chapter 9, the state mini-DOMAs have sometimes gone overboard in just the same way, cavalierly hurting people in order to make a symbolic point. Jonathan Lemmon, the pre–Civil War traveling slaveowner we met in Chapter 5, was not treated this harshly. New York would not let him keep his slaves, but a private fund-raising effort collected five thousand dollars to compensate him for the loss of his only property, and the judge who freed his slaves contributed to the fund.[5] Even with respect to slavery, the country understood that there were human beings on the other side of the issue, and that if possible, their lives should not be destroyed.

It is possible to construe most of the mini-DOMA laws narrowly and therefore avoid the danger that they be found unconstitutional. It appears that a lot of use will have to be made of this kind of narrowing device because laws that lash out wildly at gay people seem to keep getting passed.

One recent decision has turned, in part, on the attractions of a federalist solution. In its 2006 case, *Cote-Whitacre v. Dept. of Public Health*,[6] a little more than two years after it declared a right to same-sex marriage, the Massachusetts Supreme Court upheld a statute prohibiting the issuance of marriage licenses to persons whose marriages would not be recognized by their home state. The statute had been around for nearly a century but had been moribund until same-sex marriage made it relevant again. The Court had previously held that there was no rational basis for denying gays the right to marry, but it now decided that there *was* a rational basis for declining to celebrate evasive marriages. Justice Spina's plurality opinion emphasized Massachusetts's "significant interest in not meddling in matters in which another State, the one where the couple actually resides, has a paramount interest."[7] He went on to argue that "it is rational, and hopeful, for the Commonwealth to believe that if it adheres to principles of comity and respects the laws of other jurisdictions, then other jurisdictions will correspondingly respect the laws of Massachusetts and recognize same-sex marriages of Massachusetts couples lawfully celebrated in this Commonwealth."[8]

The anti-evasion statute, enacted in 1913 and based on the Uniform Marriage Evasion Act (discussed on p. 87, above), is a clumsy statute, reflecting a crudely mechanical approach to choice of law that has since been superseded. As we saw in Chapter 6, even evasive marriages have sometimes been recognized by modern courts. The statute assumes that, in choice of law cases, foreign marriages either are or are not recognized, for all purposes. The possibility that different incidents of marriage might involve different policies was not considered.[9] But the Court's more general approach to the problem is reasonable. Massachusetts will respect other states' laws and expect similar treatment from them.

More nuanced conflicts rules, of the kind that I have been proposing in this book, will not make everyone happy. They may not make *anyone* happy. Neither side gets the total victory it seeks. But the approach advocated here does accommodate the most pressing interests on both sides. It is the least bad answer to the problem.

So why would anyone support it?

Same-sex marriage is not likely to spread very widely in the United States in the near future. Public opinion is too strongly against it. But there are signs that this will change. Polls reflect a generational divide on the issue: while most Americans oppose it, most eighteen- to twenty-nine-year-olds are in favor.[10] The long-term hopes of the same-sex marriage movement are its best reason not to overreach, and to accept more modest victories. They are also perhaps the most powerful reason why opponents are so eager to cement their position into the law now, while political forces still favor them.

As for those who oppose same-sex marriage, their position is most powerful when they are careful to dissociate themselves from bigotry and hysteria. In particular, they need to be more discriminating about which legal rules they will advocate. They should oppose same-sex marriage, of course, but they should also oppose the kind of broad antigay legislation such as that in Florida and Virginia.

What we need is competition of a benign sort. Each side should intensely compete to show that it is more reasonable than the other. At a minimum, we should not respond to our disagreements in a *less* civilized and humane way than we managed to do in the shameful days of racial segregation.

Notes

Introduction

Epigraph. Estin v. Estin, 334 U.S. 541, 553 (1948) (Jackson, J., dissenting).

1. See Hayden Curry et al., *A Legal Guide for Gay and Lesbian Couples* (12th ed. 2004); Harold L. Lustig, *Four Steps to Financial Security for Lesbian and Gay Couples* (1999); Frederick Hertz, *Legal Affairs: Essential Advice for Same-Sex Couples* (1998); Nan D. Hunter et al., *The Rights of Lesbians, Gay Men, Bisexuals, and Transgender People* (4th ed. 2004).

2. I have argued in favor of same-sex marriage elsewhere; see Andrew Koppelman, *The Gay Rights Question in Contemporary American Law* 53–93 (2002). I have not changed my mind, but this book presumes that disagreement over this issue will persist.

3. *Kinney v. Commonwealth,* 71 Va. (30 Gratt.) 858, 869 (1878).

4. H. L. A. Hart, *The Concept of Law* 89 (2d ed. 1994).

5. *Id.* at 135.

Chapter 1.
How We Got Here

1. *In re Kaufmann's Will,* 20 A.D.2d 464, 247 N.Y.S.2d 664 (1964), aff'd, 15 N.Y.2d 825, 257 N.Y.S.2d 941, 205 N.E.2d 864 (1965). (All quotations are drawn from these opinions.) Walter was not left destitute. A later case indicates that "the will next in line for consideration for probate was the one giving the residual estate half to Weiss and half to [Robert's nephews]," and the estate appears to have been distributed in accordance with this will. The

parties were still fighting as late as 1972, by which time Robert's brother had expended more than $284,000 in litigation expenses. *Weiss v. Kay Jewelry Stores,* 470 F.2d 1259, 1263 (D.C. Cir. 1972). The result in the *Kaufmann* case was not unusual. See Jeffrey G. Sherman, Undue Influence and the Homosexual Testator, 42 U. Pitt. L. Rev. 225 (1981).

2. See, e.g., Sherman, Undue Influence, at 239–48; Ray D. Madoff, Unmasking Undue Influence, 81 Minn. L. Rev. 571, 592–600 (1997); Jesse Dukeminier et al., *Wills, Trusts, and Estates* 176 (7th ed. 2005). For recent cases with similar facts reaching a different result, see *Estate of Sarabia,* 270 Cal. Rptr. 560 (Cal. App. 1990); *Evans v. May,* 923 S.W.2d 712 (Tex. App. 1996).

3. These figures are summarized in Sean Cahill, *Same-Sex Marriage in the United States: Focus on the Facts* 43–46 (2004).

4. Some recent state statutes go further and might even reinstate the result in *Kaufmann,* but there is no evidence that this was intended; it is probably a consequence of careless drafting. See Chapter 9.

5. The most thorough study to date of the legal status of gays during the antigay hysteria that prevailed in the decade and a half after World War II is William N. Eskridge Jr., *Gaylaw: Challenging the Apartheid of the Closet* (1999). The purge that took place during this period within the federal government is described in David K. Johnson, *The Lavender Scare: The Cold War Persecution of Gays and Lesbians in the Federal Government* (2004). This history is recounted more briefly in George Chauncey, *Why Marriage? The History Shaping Today's Debate over Gay Equality* 5–22 (2004), and Andrew Koppelman, Why Gay Legal History Matters, 113 Harv. L. Rev. 2035 (2000).

6. See *Baker v. Nelson,* 191 N.W.2d 185 (Minn. 1971), appeal dismissed, 409 U.S. 810 (1972); *Jones v. Hallahan,* 501 S.W.2d 588 (Ky. 1973); *Singer v. Hara,* 522 P.2d 1187 (Wash. Ct. App.), review denied, 84 Wash. 2d 1008 (1974).

7. *Jones* at 589.

8. *Adams v. Howerton,* 486 F.Supp. 1119 (C.D. Calif. 1980), aff'd on other grounds, 673 F.2d 1036 (9th Cir. 1982); *De Santo v. Barnsley,* 476 A.2d 952 (Pa. Super. 1984).

9. All figures are drawn from Chauncey, *Why Marriage?,* at 48.

10. *Id.* at 98. See Chauncey's excellent discussion of why marriage became a goal of the gay movement, in *id.* at 87–136.

11. *Baehr v. Lewin,* 852 P.2d 44 (Haw. 1993).

12. *Baehr v. Miike,* 1996 Westlaw 694235, 1996 Haw. App. Lexis 138 (Haw. Cir. Ct., 1st Cir., Dec. 3, 1996).

13. DOMA is discussed in detail in Chapter 8.

14. These laws are all discussed in Chapter 9.

15. See Haw. Const., Art. 1, § 23 (enacted 1998).

16. *Baker v. State,* 744 A.2d 864 (Vt. 1999).

17. 15 V.S.A. § 1204 grants parties to a civil union "all the same benefits, protections and responsibilities under law, whether they derive from statute, administrative or court rule, policy, common law or any other source of civil law, as are granted to a spouse in a marriage."

18. 2003 Ca. A.B. 205, § 297.5(a), declares that "[r]egistered domestic partners shall have the same rights, protections, and benefits, and shall be subject to the same responsibilities, obligations, and duties under law, whether they derive from statutes, administrative regulations, court rules, government policies, common law, or any other provisions or sources of law, as are granted to and imposed upon spouses." The only distinction from Vermont is that California domestic partners, in filing state income tax returns, "shall use the same filing status as is used on their federal tax returns." *Id.,* § 297.5(g). This proviso was added because legislators feared that conflicting tax codes would make same-sex households more likely to be audited. California Domestic Partner Law Signed, *USA Today,* Sept. 20, 2003.

19. Connecticut Public Act No. 05–10, § 14, declares that "[p]arties to a civil union shall have all the same benefits, protections and responsibilities under law, whether derived from the general statutes, administrative regulations or court rules, policy, common law or any other source of civil law, as are granted to spouses in a marriage, which is defined as the union of one man and one woman."

20. For a survey, see American Bar Association Section of Family Law, A White Paper: An Analysis of the Law Regarding Same-Sex Marriage, Civil Unions, and Domestic Partnerships, 38 Fam. L. Q. 339, 379–97, 414–16 (2004). On the specific deficiencies of one such statute, see David M. Stauss, The End or Just the Beginning for Gay Rights under the New Jersey Constitution? The New Jersey Domestic Partnership Act, *Lewis v. Harris,* and the Future of Gay Rights in New Jersey, 36 Rutgers L. J. 289, 306–18 (2004).

21. At the end of 2003, the Human Rights Campaign Foundation had tracked 7,149 private employers who provided health insurance coverage to their employees' domestic partners. Of Fortune 500 companies, 200, or 40 percent, provided domestic partner benefits. As recently as 1998, the figure was 13 percent. Human Rights Campaign Foundation, The State of the Workplace for Lesbian, Gay, Bisexual and Transgender Americans, 2003 (2004).

22. *Goodridge v. Dep't of Public Health,* 798 N.E.2d 941 (Mass. 2003).

23. *In re Opinions of the Justices to the Senate,* 802 N.E. 2d 565, 570 (Mass. 2004).

24. Kees Waaldijk, Others May Follow: The Introduction of Marriage,

Quasi-Marriage, and Semi-Marriage for Same-Sex Couples in European Countries, 38 New England L. Rev. 569 (2004); Robert Wintemute and Mads Andenaes, eds., *Legal Recognition of Same-Sex Partnerships: A Study of National, European and International Law* (2001).

25. See Mark Levy, Uganda Bans Gay Marriage, 365Gay.com, Sept. 30, 2005.

26. See Carl Hulse, Senators Block Initiative to Ban Same-Sex Unions, *N.Y. Times,* July 16, 2004, at A1; Sheryl Gay Stolberg, Same-Sex Marriage Amendment Fails in House, *N.Y. Times,* Oct. 1, 2004.

27. See Carl Hulse, House Backs Bill to Limit Power of Judges, *N.Y. Times,* July 23, 2004.

28. All of these arguments are described and evaluated in greater detail in Andrew Koppelman, *The Gay Rights Question in Contemporary American Law* 6–71 (2002).

29. Daniel Pinello has shown that gay rights claims have gotten a far better reception in state than in federal courts. Daniel R. Pinello, *Gay Rights and American Law* (2003).

30. See *Lawrence v. Texas,* 539 U.S. 558, 578 (2003) ("The present case does not involve . . . whether the government must give formal recognition to any relationship that homosexual persons seek to enter"); *Id.* at 585 (O'Connor, J., concurring in the judgment) ("Texas cannot assert any legitimate state interest here, such as . . . preserving the traditional institution of marriage. Unlike the moral disapproval of same-sex relations—the asserted state interest in this case—other reasons exist to promote the institution of marriage beyond mere moral disapproval of an excluded group"). Nor are lower federal courts likely to force the Supreme Court's hand by finding a constitutional right to same-sex marriage. They are probably bound by a 1972 precedent in which the Court held that the denial of a marriage license to a same-sex couple did not present a substantial federal question. See *Wilson v. Ake,* 354 F.Supp.2d 1298 (M.D. Fla. 2005), citing *Baker v. Nelson,* 191 N.W.2d 185 (Minn. 1971), appeal dismissed, 409 U.S. 810 (1972); but see *Smelt v. County of Orange,* 374 F.Supp.2d 861, 873 n.18 (C.D. Calif. 2005); *In re Kandu,* 315 B.R. 123, 137–38 (Bkrcy. W.D. Wash. 2004).

Chapter 2.
Marriage, Choice of Law, and Public Policy

1. Actually, in the *Wilkins* case, the marriage was probably not valid even under Indiana law because Indiana also required parental consent for

sixteen-year-olds. Whoever issued the Indiana license appears to have ignored this requirement. See *Wilkins v. Zelichowski,* 140 A.2d 65, 65 (N.J. 1958).

2. See Joan Shufro, Should These Marriages Have Been Saved? Extreme Cruelty as a Cause of Action for Divorce in New Jersey 1950–1970, 23 Women's Rts. L. Rep. 79 (2001).

3. Mark P. Gergen, Equality and the Conflict of Laws, 73 Iowa L. Rev. 893, 902 (1988).

4. Beale's theory is briefly summarized in Lea Brilmayer, *Conflict of Laws* 20–25 (2d ed. 1995).

5. See Brilmayer, *Conflict of Laws* 236–37.

6. See Mark D. Rosen, Extraterritoriality and Political Heterogeneity in American Federalism, 150 U. Pa. L. Rev. 855 (2002).

7. Prosecutorial Remedies and Tools against the Exploitation of Children Abroad Act, Pub. Law 108-21, 117 Stat. 650 (2003).

8. Thanks to Joseph Singer for emphasizing this.

9. Eugene F. Scoles, Peter Hay, Patrick J. Borchers, & Symeon C. Symeonides, *Conflict of Laws* 560 (4th ed. 2004).

10. Restatement (Second) of Conflict of Laws, sec. 283(2) (1971).

11. The reporter of the Restatement (Second) stated that "[s]o far as is known, no marriages [valid where celebrated] have been held invalid . . . except by application of the law of a State where at least one of the spouses was domiciled at the time of marriage and where both made their home thereafter." Willis L. M. Reese, Marriage in American Conflict of Laws, 26 Int'l & Comp. L. Q. 952, 955 (1977).

12. *Wilkins,* 140 A.2d at 67–68.

13. 31 W. Va. 70, 8 S.E. 596 (1888).

14. Joseph Story, *Commentaries on the Conflict of Laws* 215 (8th ed. Melville Bigelow 1883).

15. Russell J. Weintraub, *Commentary on the Conflict of Laws* 104 (4th ed. 2001).

16. See Friedrich K. Juenger, *Choice of Law and Multistate Justice* 79–80 (1993).

17. Arthur Nussbaum, Public Policy and the Political Crisis in the Conflict of Laws, 49 Yale L. J. 1027, 1029 (1940).

18. *Mertz v. Mertz,* 271 N.Y. 466, 472, 3 N.E.2d 597, 599 (1936).

19. Weintraub, *Commentary on the Conflict of Laws,* at 105.

20. "What amounted to substantial dissimilarity was never quite clear. Some states held that almost any difference in the size, distribution of the claim, or even the procedure for its enforcement constituted such dissimilarity as would prevent the forum from entertaining suit. Today, the dissimilarity

rule has probably disappeared from the law, and even if it has not, the strong local public policy basis for refusing to hear out-of-state causes of action covers what is left of it." Luther L. McDougal III, Robert L. Felix, & Ralph U. Whitten, *American Conflicts Law* 158 (5th ed. 2001). On the other hand, some states seem to be reviving the rule: the Connecticut attorney general and a tax court in New Jersey both opined that, although those states recognize civil unions of gay people, they will give no effect whatsoever to Massachusetts or Canadian same-sex marriages. Opinion of Conn. Att'y Gen. Richard Blumenthal, No. 2005-024 (Sept. 20, 2005); *Hennefeld v. Montclair,* 22 N.J. Tax 166, 178–84 (2005). See Chapter 7 for discussion.

21. Scoles et al., *Conflict of Laws,* at 143–45; Weintraub, *Commentary on the Conflict of Laws* at 107–9; Restatement (Second) of Conflict of Laws, sec. 90, comment a (1972) (the rule is intended to have "only a narrow scope of application").

22. *Loucks v. Standard Oil Co.,* 224 N.Y. 99, 111, 120 N.E. 198, 202 (1918).

23. John K. Beach, Uniform Interstate Enforcement of Vested Rights, 27 Yale L. J. 656, 661–62 (1918).

24. Note, The Public Policy Concept in the Conflict of Laws, 33 Colum. L. Rev. 508, 525 n.143 (1933), quoting *Pope v. Hanke,* 155 Ill. 617, 630, 40 N.E. 839, 843 (1894).

25. Nussbaum, *Public Policy and the Political Crisis,* at 1052–55; David F. Cavers, A Critique of the Choice-of-Law Problem, 47 Harv. L. Rev. 173, 183 (1933).

26. Monrad G. Paulsen & Michael I. Sovern, "Public Policy" in the Conflict of Laws, 56 Colum. L. Rev. 969 (1956). But for an argument that courts may be motivated by less legitimate concerns, see Gary J. Simson, The Public Policy Doctrine in Choice of Law: A Reconsideration of Older Themes, 1974 Wash. U. L. Q. 391.

27. *Greenwood v. Curtis,* 6 Mass. 358, 378 (1810).

28. *Adams v. Gay,* 19 Vt. 358, 367 (1847), quoted with approval in *Swann v. Swann,* 21 Fed. 299, 305 (E.D. Ark. 1884).

29. Paulsen & Sovern, "Public Policy," at 980.

30. *Wong v. Tenneco, Inc.,* 39 Cal. 3d 126, 142 (1985) (Mosk, J., dissenting). See also Louise Weinberg, Against Comity, 80 Geo. L. J. 53, 74 (1991) (deference to foreign law "can mean accommodation to values repugnant to this country," such as anti-Semitism).

31. See *Holzer v. Deutsche Reichsbahn-Gesellschaft,* 277 N.Y. 474, 14 N.E.2d 798 (1938). For discussion of *Holzer,* see Andrew Koppelman, Same-Sex Marriage, Choice of Law, and Public Policy, 76 Tex. L. Rev. 921, 940 n.57 (1998).

32. *Williams v. North Carolina,* 317 U.S. 287, 298 (1942).

33. The hypothetical is obsolete today because no state now permits people younger than eighteen to marry without parental consent. See Richard A. Leiter, ed., National Survey of State Laws 434–38 (5th ed. 2005). On the other hand, in every state there is an age below which even parental consent will not validate a marriage, so evasion cases continue to arise. See, e.g., Jodi Wilgoren, Rape Charge Follows Marriage to a 14-Year-Old, *N.Y. Times,* Aug. 30, 2005, at A1.

34. In such a case, it may be unconstitutional to invoke the exception. See Chapter 8.

35. Nussbaum, *Public Policy and the Political Crisis,* at 1055.

36. See Douglas Laycock, Equal Citizens of Equal and Territorial States: The Constitutional Foundations of Choice of Law, 92 Colum. L. Rev. 249, 313 (1992).

37. *Id.* at 337.

38. *Estin v. Estin,* 334 U.S. 541, 553 (1948) (Jackson, J., dissenting).

Chapter 3.
Miscegenation in the Conflict of Laws

1. *State v. Ross,* 76 N.C. 242, 243 (1877).

2. *Id.* at 246.

3. *Id.*

4. *Id.* at 245.

5. *Id.* at 247.

6. *Id.*

7. *Id.* at 249 (Reade, J., dissenting).

8. *Id.* at 250.

9. *Id.* The dissenters' position never prevailed in North Carolina, where *Ross* was cited with approval (albeit in dictum) in a number of later cases. See *Woodward v. Blue,* 103 N.C. 109, 114, 9 S.E. 492 (1889); *State v. Cutshall,* 110 N.C. 538, 541, 15 S.E. 261 (1892); *Fowler v. Fowler,* 131 N.C. 169, 173, 42 S.E. 563 (1902); *Wood v. Wood,* 181 N.C. 227, 229, 106 S.E. 753 (1921); *Howard v. Howard,* 200 N.C. 574, 580, 158 S.E. 753 (1931); *Harris v. Harris,* 257 N.C. 416, 420, 126 S.E.2d 85 (1962).

10. There are also a few cases voiding marriages, valid where celebrated, on grounds of insanity. See, e.g., *Beddow v. Beddow,* 257 S.W.2d 45 (Ky. 1952); *First Nat'l Bank v. North Dakota Workmen's Compensation Bureau,* 68 N.W.2d 661 (N.D. 1955). And there was a vigorous dispute in the early 1900s

over the recognition of arranged marriages from Japan in which the immigrant bride had never met her husband. See Nancy Cott, *Public Vows: A History of Marriage and the Nation* 149–54 (2000).

11. 2 Albert A. Ehrenzweig & Erik Jayme, *Private International Law* 166 (1973). See, e.g., *Compo v. Jackson Iron Co.,* 50 Mich. 578, 16 N.W. 295 (1883); *Kobogum v. Jackson Iron Co.,* 76 Mich. 498, 507–08, 43 N.W. 602 (1889); *Oklahoma Land Co. v. Thomas,* 34 Okla. 681, 127 P. 8 (1912); *Pompey v. King,* 101 Okla. 253, 225 P. 175 (1923); see generally G. W. Bartholemew, Recognition of Polygamous Marriages in America, 13 Int'l & Comp. L. Q. 1022 (1964). These cases were rare, however. "The federal government consistently encouraged or forced Indians to adopt Christian-model monogamy as the *sine qua non* of civilization and morality." Cott, *Public Vows,* at 26; see also *id.* at 121–23.

12. See Edwin Brown Firmage & Richard Collin Mangrum, *Zion in the Courts: A Legal History of the Church of Jesus Christ of Latter-Day Saints,* 1830–1900, at 322–36 (1988); Bartholemew, Recognition of Polygamous Marriages, at 1030–31, 1067–68.

13. Even today, when polygamy continues to be practiced by some dissenting Mormon communities on the Arizona-Colorado border, it is their practice for the husband to civilly marry only the first wife, thereby remaining technically obedient to the prohibition of polygamy.

14. See Hendrik Hartog, *Man and Wife in America: A History* 70–73, 256–58, 278–82 (2000).

15. Lennart Palsson, *Marriage in Comparative Conflict of Laws: Substantive Conditions* 41–55 (1981); Eugene F. Scoles, Peter Hay, Patrick J. Borchers, & Symeon C. Symeonides, *Conflict of Laws* 573–77 (4th ed. 2004); Annotation, Inhibition by Decree of Divorce, or Statute of State or Country in Which It Is Granted, against Remarriage, as Affecting a Marriage Celebrated in Another State or Country, 32 A.L.R. 1116 (1924); Annotation, Extraterritorial Effect of Divorce Decree or Statute Prohibiting Remarriage of Party or Parties, 1918E Ann. Cas. 1074.

16. *People v. Kay,* 141 Misc. 574, 252 N.Y.S. 518 (1931) (husband in polyandrous marriage, valid in Turkey, not liable for support and maintenance of wife in New York); *Ng Suey Hi v. Weedin,* 21 F.2d 801 (9th Cir. 1929) (U.S. citizen's daughter, born in China of a polygamous marriage, not entitled to be admitted to United States as a citizen).

17. See *In re Dalip Singh Bir's Estate,* 188 P.2d 499 (Cal. Ct. App. 1948) (allowing both wives in a polygamous marriage to share husband's estate); *Royal v. Cudahy Packing Co.,* 195 Iowa 759, 190 N.W. 427 (1922) (allowing recognition of marriage, potentially polygamous under Mohammedan law, that was in fact monogamous); see generally Ernest G. Lorenzen, Comment,

Polygamy and the Conflict of Laws, 32 Yale L. J. 471 (1923); Annotation, Recognition of Foreign Marriage as Affected by the Conditions or Manner of Dissolving It under the Foreign Law, or the Toleration of Polygamous Marriages, 74 A.L.R. 1533 (1931). One early court went so far as to suggest in dictum that "[i]f a Turk with his two wives were to come here, we would administer to them the justice due to the relations contracted by them at home." *Williams v. Oates,* 27 N.C. 439, 444, 5 Iredale 535 (1845) (Ruffin, C. J.).

18. See Palsson, *Marriage in Comparative Conflict of Laws,* at 75–76.

19. See *State v. Brown,* 47 Ohio St. 102, 23 N.E. 747 (1890) (prosecution of uncle for intercourse with niece); see also *United States ex rel. Devine v. Rodgers,* 109 F. 886 (D.C. 1901) (niece, validly married in Russia to uncle who later became naturalized U.S. citizen, could not remain in United States as his wife); *Osoinach v. Watkins,* 235 Ala. 564, 569, 180 So. 577, 117 A.L.R. 179 (1938) (voiding, for inheritance purposes, marriage of nephew to widow of his deceased uncle) ("The Legislature is fully competent to declare what marriages shall be void in its own state, notwithstanding their validity in the state where celebrated, whether contracted between parties who were in good faith domiciled in the state where the ceremony was performed, or between parties who left the state of domicile for the purpose of avoiding its statute, when they come or return to the state"). But see, e.g., *Garcia v. Garcia,* 25 S.D. 645, 652, 127 N.W. 586 (1910) (first cousin marriage could not be annulled); *Sutton v. Warren,* 10 Met. (Mass.) 451 (1845) (allowing litigant to plead marriage to his aunt in a suit on a promissory note given to her). Some early cases even sustained marriages of their domiciliaries contracted outside the state in evasion of the forum's restrictions. See, e.g., *Stevenson v. Gray,* 56 Ky. (17 B.Mon.) 193 (1856) (nephew and uncle's wife).

20. See *Loving v. Virginia,* 388 U.S. 1 (1967).

21. The following discussion is in part a compression of Andrew Koppelman, Why Discrimination against Lesbians and Gay Men Is Sex Discrimination, 69 N.Y.U. L. Rev. 197, 220–34 (1994).

22. This is always potentially a problem with intermarriage in stratified societies. See Kingsley Davis, Intermarriage in Caste Societies, 43 Am. Anthropologist 376 (1941).

23. This is illustrated with particular clarity by Virginia in the 1600s, where the question of the status of biracial children was an urgent and unsettled issue. The first statute prohibiting interracial sex quickly followed. Charles Frank Robinson II, *Dangerous Liaisons: Sex and Love in the Segregated South* 2–5 (2003).

24. "Fear of miscegenation permeates virtually all of the racist literature of post–Civil War America." 7 *Anti-Black Thought, 1863–1925, Racial*

Determinism and the Fear of Miscegenation, Pre-1900, at xxvi (John David Smith ed., 1993). It has remained prominent in racist hate literature. See Charles H. Stember, *Sexual Racism: The Emotional Barrier to an Integrated Society* 15–32 (1976). The miscegenation taboo was commonly given a religious justification, so that violation of the prohibition was understood to mean defiance of the will of God. See Jane Dailey, Sex, Segregation, and the Sacred after *Brown,* 91 J. Am. Hist. 119 (2004); Forrest G. Wood, *The Arrogance of Faith: Christianity and Race in America from the Colonial Era to the Twentieth Century* (1990).

25. On the history of lynching in the United States, see Philip Dray, *At the Hands of Persons Unknown: The Lynching of Black America* (2002); Martha Hodes, *White Women, Black Men: Illicit Sex in the Nineteenth-Century South* 176–208 (1997).

26. Joel Kovel, *White Racism: A Psychohistory* 67 (2d ed. 1984). This mythology was an important part of the ideology supporting lynching, even though most of the lynchings that actually took place were not motivated by allegations of rape. See Nell I. Painter, "Social Equality," Miscegenation, Labor, and Power, in *The Evolution of Southern Culture* 47, 53 (Numan V. Bartley ed., 1988); Joel Williamson, *The Crucible of Race: Black-White Relations in the American South Since Emancipation* 183–89 (1984).

27. The courts shared this hypersensitivity to black male sexuality. See, e.g., *McQuirter v. State,* 63 So. 2d 388 (Ala. Ct. App. 1953) (sustaining conviction, for attempted assault with intent to rape, of a black man who stared at a white woman and followed her down a street).

28. Quoted in Robert J. Sickels, *Race, Marriage, and the Law* 32 (1972).

29. W. J. Cash, *The Mind of the South* 115 (1941).

30. The various theories are surveyed in Sickels, *Race, Marriage, and the Law,* at 10–31; Stember, *Sexual Racism,* at 37–89.

31. John Dollard, *Caste and Class in a Southern Town* 137 (3d ed. 1957).

32. Calvin C. Hernton, *Sex and Racism in America* 24 (1966).

33. Kovel, *White Racism,* at 71–72.

34. See Juan Williams, *Eyes on the Prize: America's Civil Rights Years, 1954–1965,* at 37–57 (1987).

35. *Kinney v. Commonwealth,* 71 Va. (30 Gratt.) 858, 869 (1878). Similar statements by leading legal authorities in the southern courts are ubiquitous. See, e.g., *Pace v. State,* 69 Ala. 231, 232 (1881) ("Its result may be the amalgamation of the two races, producing a mongrel population and a degraded civilization, the prevention of which is dictated by a sound public policy affecting the highest interests of society and government"); *Green v. State,* 58 Ala. 190, 195 (1877) ("And surely there can not be any tyranny or injustice in

requiring both [races] alike, to form this union with those of their own race only, whom God hath joined together by indelible peculiarities, which declare that He has made the two races distinct"); *State v. Gibson*, 36 Ind. 389, 404 (1871) ("The natural law, which forbids their intermarriage and that amalgamation which leads to a corruption of races, is as clearly divine as that which imparted to them different natures") (quoting *West Chester & Philadelphia R.R. v. Miles*, 55 Pa. 209, 213 [1867]); *Pennegar v. State*, 10 S.W. 305 (Tenn. 1889) (referring to "the very pronounced convictions of the people of this State as to the demoralization and debauchery involved in such alliances"); *Naim v. Naim*, 87 S.E.2d 749, 756 (Va. 1955) (arguing that the state's legitimate purposes in prohibiting miscegenation are "to preserve the racial integrity of its citizens" and to prevent "the corruption of the blood," "a mongrel breed of citizens," and "the obliteration of racial pride"); see also W. C. Rodgers, *A Treatise on the Law of Domestic Relations* 49 (1899) (describing the purpose of miscegenation laws as "to keep pure and unmixed the blood of the two races, to the end that the paramount excellence of the one may not be lowered by an admixture with the other").

36. For cases reversing convictions on this basis, see *Metcalf v. State*, 16 Ala. App. 389, 78 So. 305 (1918); *Hovis v. State*, 257 S.W. 363 (Ark. 1924); *Wilson v. State*, 13 S.W.2d 24 (Ark. 1929); *Jackson v. State*, 129 So. 306 (Ala. App. 1930); *Gilbert v. State*, 23 So.2d 22 (Ala. App. 1945); *Wildman v. State*, 25 So.2d 808 (Fla. 1946); *Poland v. State*, 339 S.W.2d 421 (Ark. 1960); *Hardin v. State*, 339 S.W.2d 423 (Ark. 1960). A conviction was affirmed, on evidence that the couple had lived together for many years, in *Parramore v. State*, 81 Fla. 621, 88 So. 472 (1921). See also *State v. Brown*, 236 La. 562, 108 So.2d 233, 235 (1959) (statute prohibits "customary or repeated acts of sexual intercourse, and not merely an isolated case of intercourse").

37. See *Moore v. State*, 7 Tex. App. 608, 609 (1880) ("the fact of marriage is an essential ingredient, and must be positively averred and proved.... A mere cohabitation within this State, without a previous intermarriage, does not bring the offence within the statute"); *Frasher v. State*, 3 Tex. App. 263, 280 (1877) (marriage certificate was properly admitted in evidence).

38. See *Williams v. State*, 125 So. 690 (Ala. Ct. App. 1930). In general, interracial sexual relations were less likely to be prosecuted to the extent that they appeared casual and unequal. For numerous illustrations, see Robinson, *Dangerous Liaisons.*

39. *Ex parte Kinney*, 14 F. Cas. 602 (C.C.E.D. Va. 1879) (No. 7825).

40. See Peter Wallenstein, *Tell the Court I Love My Wife: Race, Marriage, and Law—An American History* 110 (2002) (citing Virginia prison records).

41. *Loving v. Commonwealth,* 206 Va. 924, 147 S.E.2d 78 (1966), rev'd, 388 U.S. 1 (1967); *Naim v. Naim,* 197 Va. 80, 87 S.E.2d 749 (1955), vacated and remanded, 350 U.S. 891 (1955), on remand, 197 Va. 734, 90 S.E.2d 849 (1956), appeal dismissed, 350 U.S. 985 (1956); *Stevens v. United States,* 146 F.2d 120 (10th Cir. 1944) (applying Oklahoma law); *In re Takahashi's Estate,* 113 Mont. 490, 129 P.2d 217 (1942); *Baker v. Carter,* 180 Okla. 71, 68 P.2d 85 (1937); *Eggers v. Olson,* 104 Okla. 297, 301, 231 P. 483 (1924); *Gabisso's Succession,* 119 La. 704, 44 So. 438 (1907); *Walker's Estate,* 5 Ariz. 70, 46 P. 67 (1896); *In re Wilbur's Estate,* 8 Wash. 35, 35 P. 407 (1894); *Georgia v. Tutty,* 41 F. 753 (C.C.Ga. 1890); *Greenhow v. James,* 80 Va. 636, 641 (1885); *Kinney v. Commonwealth,* 71 Va. (30 Gratt.) 858, 869 (1878); *State v. Kennedy,* 76 N.C. 251 (1877); *Dupre v. Boulard,* 10 La. Ann. 411 (1855).

42. 16 Mass. 157 (1819).

43. *Id.* at 160.

44. *Id.* at 160–61.

45. *Id.* at 161.

46. Joseph Story, *Commentaries on the Conflict of Laws* 206–07 (8th ed. Melville Bigelow 1883).

47. See *Id.* at 225–26 (collecting sources).

48. *Medway* is called "directly in point" and cited favorably in *Garcia v. Garcia,* 25 S.D. 645, 652, 127 N.W. 586 (1910), but this case, involving a marriage between first cousins that was valid where it was contracted and where they were then domiciled, involved neither evasion nor miscegenation. An evasive interracial marriage was also sustained in *State v. Hand,* 87 Neb. 189, 126 N.W. 1002, 28 L.R.A. (N.S.) 753 (1910), but Nebraska had a statute stating that all marriages contracted outside the state, which were valid where celebrated, were valid in Nebraska. *People v. Wilkerson,* 278 P. 466 (Cal. Dist. Ct. App. 1929) reversed a conviction for contributing to the delinquency of a minor. The defendant, a black man, had encouraged an eighteen-year-old white woman to leave her parents and travel with him to Mexico, where they married. "Being a white woman, according to our statutes it would have been unlawful for her to have married a negro in this state," the court noted, "but it is not here suggested or intimated that any legal obstacle prevented the consummation of a marriage between the girl and defendant in the republic of Mexico." *Id.* at 467. The question of the marriage's continuing validity in California was not presented.

49. Mass. Rev. Stats. 1836, c. 75, s. 6, Pub. Stats. c. 145, s. 10; cited in Story, *Commentaries on the Conflict of Laws,* at 225.

50. *Miller v. Lucks,* 36 So. 2d 140, 142 (Miss. 1948).

51. *Caballero v. Executor,* 24 La. Ann. 573, 575 (1872).

52. *Whittington v. McCaskill,* 65 Fla. 162, 165, 61 So. 236, 237 (1913).

53. H. R. Hahlo, *The South African Law of Husband and Wife* 63 (3d. ed. 1969). Oddly, the foreign restriction applied only to males: "A woman who is a South African citizen or domiciled in the Republic may, apparently, validly contract a mixed marriage outside the Republic." *Id.* at 63–64. A fortiori, a person of either sex who was neither domiciled in nor a citizen of South Africa could do so.

54. The laws were amended where this seemed necessary to achieve this object. The act originally applied only to domiciliaries of South Africa but was amended in 1968 to include citizens. "The object of the amendment was to prevent two persons, citizens but not domiciliaries of South Africa, one of whom was a European and the other a Non-European, concluding a marriage abroad that was valid by the *lex loci celebrationis,* and then claiming the right to be readmitted to South Africa and live together." *Id.* at 580.

Owing to ambiguities in South Africa's race laws, even citizens who had been officially classified by the government as being of different races managed successfully on occasion to evade the law's restrictions. One couple, after being denied reclassification, emigrated to England, married there and stayed there for some time, and later returned to South Africa. On appeal, the court quashed their criminal convictions, holding that the government's classifications were not necessarily conclusive in such prosecutions. *S. v. F. and Another,* 1970 (2) S.A. 484 (T). One South African commentator concluded that this approach was necessitated by practical exigency: "For it would be unreasonable to expect a person bent upon gratification of his sexual desires to require production of an identity document as a passport to pleasure." P. Q. R. Boberg, *The Law of Persons and the Family* 129 (1977).

55. Translated and quoted in S. W. D. Rowson, Some Private International Law Problems Arising Out of European Racial Legislation, 1933–1945, 10 Modern L. Rev. 345, 346 (1947).

56. Max-Planck-Institut fur Auslandisches und Internationales Privatrecht, Die deutsche Rechtsprechung auf dem Gebiete des Interationalen Privatrechts in den Jahren 1935 bis 1944, Band I 30–32 (1980). I am grateful to Jon Pratter, international law librarian at the University of Texas Law Library, for finding and translating this case.

57. See Jurisdiction over Nationals Abroad (Germany) Case, 9 Ann. Dig. and Rep. Pub. Int'l L. Cas., 1938–40, at 294–97.

58. Act 180 of 1906, in 1 Constitution and Statutes of Louisiana 397–98 (1920); see also La. Rev. Civ. Code (1925) Art. 95 (citing statute).

59. Tex. Penal Code Ann. Art. 326 (Vernon 1879) (emphasis added).

60. The Louisiana and Texas laws are the only relevant statutes that

were found in a comprehensive survey in 1927. See Note, Intermarriage with Negroes—A Survey of State Statutes, 36 Yale L. J. 858, 864–65 n.25 (1927).

61. 36 Tex. 68 (1871).

62. The history of Texas miscegenation statutes is briefly described in Andrew Koppelman, Same-Sex Marriage, Choice of Law, and Public Policy, 76 Tex. L. Rev. 921, 956 n.121 (1998).

63. *Id.* at 69.

64. *In re Morgan's Estate,* 203 Cal. 569, 575, 265 P. 241, 244 (1928).

65. Louisiana Code of 1825, Art. 95.

66. 66 Tenn. (7 Baxter) 9, 10–11 (1872).

67. The reported *Bell* case does not state the parties' domicile, but the same court later described the case as one "where the parties were domiciled in Mississippi at the time of the marriage." *Pennegar v. State,* 10 S.W. 305, 307 (Tenn. 1889).

68. *Bell,* 66 Tenn. at 11. It has been suggested that the difference in results was influenced, to some extent, by politics: by the time of the *Bell* decision, the Democrats held a clear majority in the Tennessee legislature, and Reconstruction was over. Robinson, *Dangerous Liaisons,* at 39–40. On the other hand, the *Ross* court reached the opposite result, even though Reconstruction had been dead for years in North Carolina. See Eric Foner, *Reconstruction: America's Unfinished Revolution 1863–1877,* at 440–41 (1988).

69. *Yarborough v. Yarborough,* 290 U.S. 202, 218 (1933) (Stone, J., dissenting). The only other discussion of the case in a Supreme Court decision is *Williams v. North Carolina,* 325 U.S. 226, 265 (1945) (Black, J., dissenting) (noting that the convictions in *Bell* "were not approved by this Court"). The case was followed in Tennessee courts, but it was never again invoked in a miscegenation case. See *Newman v. Kimbrough,* 59 S.W. 1061, 1063 (Tenn. Chancery 1900) (voiding remarriage in Texas after Tennessee divorce); *Rhodes v. McAfee,* 224 Tenn. (2 Pack) 495, 499–500, 457 S.W. 522 (1970) (voiding Mississippi marriage of stepfather to stepdaughter).

70. Herbert F. Goodrich, *Handbook of the Conflict of Laws* 266 (1927).

71. 47 Ohio St. 102, 23 N.E. 747 (1890).

72. 23 N.E. at 750.

73. The position of the *Ross* court is adopted in dicta in three California cases, but in none of them was continued interracial cohabitation a possibility. In *Pearson v. Pearson,* 51 Cal. 120, 124 (1875), in which a marriage in Utah, where there was "no law . . . interdicting intermarriage between white and black persons," was held valid in California, the issue was whether the widow could inherit. *People v. Godines,* 62 P.2d 787 (Cal. 1936), involved a claim of annulment for fraud on grounds that the husband, a Filipino, had told the

wife he was a Spaniard. The court said in dictum that "the marriage in question took place in New Mexico, where it was valid, and hence of itself the ethnological status of the parties was not a ground of annulment." *Id.* at 788. In *Estate of Mackay,* 3 Coffey's Prob. Dec. 318 (Cal. Dep't Super. Ct. 1894), the court found insufficient evidence that the interracial couple had married in New York, but conceded that "if it be shown by trustworthy testimony that such relation, however repugnant to our laws, had its origin in a manner and by a mode conformable to the statutes of another sovereign state, the courts of California are bound to respect it and to treat it as if it were not contrary to our code." *Id.* at 321. See also *Guirado v. Lee (In re Monk's Estate),* 120 P.2d 167 (Cal. Dist. Ct. App. 1941) (holding a marriage in Arizona of California domiciliaries void under an Arizona statute). In *Guirado,* had California law been dispositive, there would have been no need to examine the Arizona rule. Stronger authority for the *Ross* court's position can be found in *Briten v. Jorgensen (In re Takahashi's Estate),* 129 P.2d 217 (Mont. 1942), which authoritatively construed a statute invalidating any interracial marriage outside the state "by any person who has, prior to the time of contracting or solemnizing said marriage, been a resident of the state of Montana." *Id.* at 220 (quoting act of Mar. 3, 1909, ch. 49, 1909 Mont. Laws 57–58 [repealed 1953]). The court held: "It is clear that it was not intended to apply generally to non-residents, and there is no reason to believe that the legislature intended to single out non-residents who had formerly resided in the state as being controlled by the law. The more reasonable view is that the language employed in speaking of prior residence in the state was intended to have the more restricted meaning as applying to the prior time immediately preceding the marriage." *Id.*

74. 14 F. Cas. 602 (C.C.E.D. Va. 1879) (No. 7825).

75. *Id.* at 606.

76. *Id.*

77. A similar, but much broader, "grandfathering" rule was part of Colorado's early miscegenation law, which declared the marriages of whites with blacks or mulattoes "absolutely void . . . Provided that nothing in this section shall be so construed as to prevent the people living in that portion of the state acquired from Mexico from marrying according to the custom of that country." L. Colo. Ter. 1864, p. 108, sec. 2, quoted in *Jackson v. City and County of Denver,* 109 Colo. 196, 197, 124 P.2d 240 (1942).

78. *Scott v. Epperson,* 141 Okla. 41, 44 (1930). Accord *Minor v. Young,* 149 La. 583, 587, 89 So. 757 (1920); *Illinois Land and Loan Co. v. Bonner,* 75 Ill. 315, 319–20 (1874).

79. *Epperson* at 44.

80. See 1 Chester G. Vernier, *American Family Laws* 204–9 (1931)

(compiling statutes). For earlier surveys to the same effect, see Note, Intermarriage with Negroes—A Survey of State Statutes, 36 Yale L. J. 858 (1927); 1 F. J. Stimson, *American Statute Law* 667–69 (1886).

81. Two recent examples, involving common law marriages that were as such invalid under forum law but were nonetheless recognized, are *Allen v. Storer*, 600 N.E.2d 1263 (Ill. App. 4th Dist. 1992), and *Johnson v. Lincoln Square Properties*, 571 So.2d 541 (Fla. App. 2d Dist. 1990).

82. See Hartog, *Man and Wife in America*, at 29–39.

83. Phyl Newbeck, *Virginia Hasn't Always Been for Lovers: Interracial Marriage Bans and the Case of Richard and Mildred Loving* 57–58 (2004). Newbeck's account does not say which of the spouses was black and which was white.

Chapter 4.
The Stakes

1. 539 U.S. 558 (2003).

2. See Tobias Barrington Wolff, Interest Analysis in Interjurisdictional Marriage Disputes, 153 U. Pa. L. Rev. 2195 (2005). Wolff also thinks that states cannot legitimately indicate their moral disapproval of same-sex relationships. I am unpersuaded. (For a different reading of the cases on which he bases this conclusion, see Chapter 5.) If he were right, then why would states be permitted to ban same-sex marriage even for their own citizens?

3. Divisions over the moral status of homosexual conduct have produced major controversies among Presbyterians, Lutherans, Episcopalians, and Methodists. See Out of the Fold? The Debate over Gay Ordination and Same-Sex Unions Poses a Critical Choice for Mainline Protestants: Embrace or Schism?, *Time*, July 3, 2000; Presbyterian Church Faces Split over Same-Sex Unions, *Buffalo News*, Mar. 12, 2001, at B1; Lutherans Address Same-Sex Unions, *Milwaukee Journal Sentinel*, Jan. 16, 2001, at 1B; Caryle Murphy, Confrontation Reveals Episcopal Split; Conservatives Attempt to Develop a Parallel, Supportive Church Hierarchy, *Wash. Post*, June 2, 2001, at B9; John Rivera, Deep and Difficult Differences Trouble Episcopalians in U.S., *Baltimore Sun*, Nov. 4, 2001, at 1F; Bruce Nolan, Methodist Split Not Seen as Answer, Bishop Says, but Church Still Deeply Divided on Gay Issue, *New Orleans Times-Picayune*, May 15, 2004. There is also a danger of schism over the issue within the worldwide Anglican Church. See Stephen Bates, *A Church at War: Anglicans and Homosexuality* (2004).

4. This position is often presented in frankly religious form, but it has

been developed as an argument that does not depend on any religious premise, most carefully by Germain Grisez, John Finnis, Robert George, Gerard Bradley, and Patrick Lee. For elaboration and critique, see Andrew Koppelman, The Decline and Fall of the Case against Same-Sex Marriage, 2 U. of St. Thomas L. J. 5, 16–25 (2004).

5. Maggie Gallagher, A Reality Waiting to Happen: A Response to Evan Wolfson, in *Marriage and Same-Sex Unions: A Debate* 12 (Lynn Wardle et al., eds., 2003).

6. Maggie Gallagher, Normal Marriage: Two Views, in *Marriage and Same-Sex Unions, supra* at 13.

7. Gallagher, A Reality Waiting to Happen, at 12. For critique of this argument, see Koppelman, Decline and Fall, at 25–31; for a rejoinder, see Maggie Gallagher, (How) Will Gay Marriage Weaken Marriage as a Social Institution: A Reply to Andrew Koppelman, 2 U. of St. Thomas L. J. 33 (2004).

8. A Time/CNN poll in February 2004 found that 62 percent of respondents opposed same-sex marriage, with 30 percent in favor. John Cloud, The Battle over Gay Marriage, *Time*, Feb. 16, 2004, at 57. In the same poll, only 51 percent of respondents thought that a homosexual relationship between consenting adults is morally wrong; 45 percent thought that it was not a moral issue. *Id.*

9. See Judith Stacey & Timothy J. Biblarz, (How) Does the Sexual Orientation of Parents Matter?, 66 Am. Soc. Rev. 159 (2001).

10. Here I borrow an analogy by Mary Anne Case. See Mary Anne Case, Marriage Licenses, 89 Minn. L. Rev. 1758 (2005); Mary Anne Case & Paul Mahoney, The Role of the State in Marriage and Corporations (unpublished ms., 1996). The analogy is also developed in Larry E. Ribstein, A Standard Form Approach to Same-Sex Marriage, 38 Creighton L. Rev. 309 (2005), and Erin A. O'Hara and Larry E. Ribstein, From Politics to Efficiency in Choice of Law, 67 U. Chi. L. Rev. 1151, 1208–10 (2000).

11. See American Bar Association Section of Family Law, A White Paper: An Analysis of the Law Regarding Same-Sex Marriage, Civil Unions, and Domestic Partnerships, 38 Fam. L. Q. 339, 407–12 (2004); Kees Waaldijk, Others May Follow: The Introduction of Marriage, Quasi-Marriage, and Semi-Marriage for Same-Sex Couples in European Countries, 38 New England L. Rev. 569 (2004); Robert Wintemute & Mads Andenaes, eds., *Legal Recognition of Same-Sex Partnerships: A Study of National, European and International Law* (2001); Mark Harper et al., *Civil Partnership: The New Law* (2005); *Minister of Home Affairs v. Fourie,* CCT 60/04 (S.A. Const. Ct. Dec. 1, 2005).

12. A poll in March 2000 found that health insurance for gay partners

was supported by 58 percent of Americans, and 54 percent thought—contrary to the federal Defense of Marriage Act—that partners should get Social Security benefits. (Only 34 percent of those polled thought there should be legally sanctioned same-sex marriages.) John Leland, Shades of Gay, *Newsweek* 46, 46 (Mar. 20, 2000). An Associated Press poll two months later produced nearly identical results. The poll found that 51 percent were opposed to allowing gay couples to marry, and 34 percent approved. On the other hand, at least half of Americans support the rights of gays to receive health insurance (53 percent), Social Security benefits (50 percent), and inheritance (56 percent) from their partners. Will Lester, Poll: Americans Back Some Gay Rights, Associated Press, May 31, 2000. When people are asked about giving gay couples *all* the same legal rights as heterosexual married couples, the split is one-third in favor, one-third against, and one-third who don't care. More precisely, when asked "Do you think gay or lesbian couples should—or should not—be allowed all the same legal rights as married couples in every state, or does it not matter to you?" the numbers are 32 percent yes, 35 percent no, and 32 percent "doesn't matter." The margin of sampling error is 3 percentage points, so the differences are statistically insignificant. The poll was conducted jointly by CNN, *USA Today,* and Gallup in September 2003. See Heather Mason, How Would Same-Sex Marriages Affect Society?, http://www.gallup.com/poll/content/login.aspx?ci=9670 (accessed Nov. 11, 2003).

13. See Vt. Stat. Ann. tit. 15, § 1204(a); Cal. Assembly 205, 2003 Reg. Sess.

14. There has been some litigation over the legislation, but that has also gotten little press. See Jim Wasserman, Conservatives Tell Court Partner Rights Are Illegal, *Contra Costa Times* (Walnut Creek, Calif.), Mar. 26, 2005, at F4; *Knight v. Superior Court,* 26 Cal. Rptr. 3d 687 (Cal. App. 3d dist. 2005).

15. See especially Evan Wolfson, *Why Marriage Matters: America, Equality, and Gay People's Right to Marry* 125–44 (2004).

16. See Andrew Koppelman, *The Gay Rights Question in Contemporary American Law* 77–79 (2002).

17. *Opinions of the Justices to the Senate,* 802 N.E.2d 565, 570 (Mass. 2004).

18. Jennifer Lee, Congressman Says Bush Is Open to States' Bolstering Gay Rights, *N.Y. Times,* Feb. 9, 2004.

19. 100 U.S. 303, 308 (1880).

20. *Id.*

21. *Plessy v. Ferguson,* 163 U.S. 537, 551 (1896).

22. 347 U.S. 483, 494 (1954).

23. It is where I think the weight of the argument inclines; see Kop-

pelman, *The Gay Rights Question*, at 53–71; but for the purposes of this book, I am setting that aside. The conflicts analysis presumes that each state is entitled to its own public policy. I am therefore construing the public policies of the states with mini-DOMAs in the most charitable way possible.

24. In a survey of anti gay violence and harassment in eight major cities, "86.2% of the gay men and women surveyed stated that they had been attacked verbally; 44.2% reported that they had been threatened with violence; 27.3% had had objects thrown at them; 34.9% had been chased or followed; 13.9% had been spit at; 19.2% had been punched, hit, kicked, or beaten; 9.3% had been assaulted with a weapon; 18.5% had been the victims of property vandalism or arson; 30.9% reported sexual harassment, many by members of their own families or by the police." National Gay Task Force, Anti-Gay/Lesbian Victimization 24 (June 1984). These results have been replicated in other studies. See Kevin T. Berrill, Anti-Gay Violence and Victimization in the United States: An Overview, in Gregory M. Herek & Kevin Berrill, eds., *Hate Crimes: Confronting Violence Against Lesbians and Gay Men* 19–45 (1992); Gary David Comstock, *Violence against Lesbians and Gay Men* (1991). A study commissioned by the National Institute of Justice, the research arm of the U.S. Department of Justice, found that gays "are probably the most frequent victims [of hate violence today]." Peter Finn & Taylor McNeil, *The Response of the Criminal Justice System to Bias Crime: An Exploratory Review* 2 (1987).

25. Amnesty International USA, *Stonewalled: Police Abuse and Misconduct against Lesbian, Gay, Bisexual and Transgender People in the U.S.* (2005).

26. American Association of University Women, *Hostile Hallways: The AAUW Survey on Sexual Harassment in America's Schools* 20, 23 (1993). See also Deborah Brake, The Cruelest of the Gender Police: Student-to-Student Sexual Harassment and Anti-Gay Peer Harassment under Title IX, 1 Geo. J. Gender & L. 37 (1999).

27. William Marsiglio, Attitudes Toward Homosexual Activity and Gays as Friends: A National Survey of Heterosexual 15- to 19-Year-Old Males, 30 J. Sex Res. 12 (1993).

28. See Safe Schools Coalition of Washington State, They Don't Even Know Me: Understanding Anti-Gay Harassment and Violence in the Schools (1999), at http://www.safeschools-wa.org/theydontevenknowme.pdf. See also Gay, Lesbian, and Straight Educational Network, The 2003 National School Climate Survey, at http://www.glsen.org/binary-data/GLSEN_ATTACHMENTS/file/300-3.PDF; Human Rights Watch, Hatred in the Hallways: Discrimination and Violence against Lesbian, Gay, Bisexual and Transgender Students in U.S. Public Schools, at http://www.hrw.org/reports/2001/

uslgbt/; Margaret Schneider, ed., *Pride and Prejudice: Working with Lesbian, Gay and Bisexual Youth* (1997); *Flores v. Morgan Hill Unified School Dist.,* 324 F.3d 1130 (2003); *Massey v. Banning Unified School Dist.,* 256 F.Supp. 2d 1090 (C.D. Cal. 2003).

29. See Andrew Koppelman, *Romer v. Evans* and Invidious Intent, 6 Wm. & Mary Bill of Rts. J. 89, 125 (1997) (quoting Gordon W. Allport, *The Nature of Prejudice* 14, 49, 57, 59 [1954]).

30. Kenneth Sherrill, The Political Power of Lesbians, Gays, and Bisexuals, PS 469, 470 (1996).

31. *Id.*

32. Morris P. Fiorina et al., *Culture War? The Myth of Polarized America* 84 (2005).

33. See Jerry Kang, Trojan Horses of Race, 118 Harv. L. Rev. 1489 (2005); Tali Mendelberg, *The Race Card: Campaign Strategy, Implicit Messages, and the Norm of Equality* (2001).

34. Richard Mohr, *The Long Arc of Justice: Lesbian and Gay Marriage, Equality, and Rights* 78 (2005).

35. Quoted in Jules Witcover, *Marathon: The Pursuit of the Presidency, 1972–1976,* at 603 (1978).

36. Kwame Anthony Appiah, *In My Father's House: Africa in the Philosophy of Culture* 14 (1992).

37. See, e.g., Congregation for the Doctrine of the Faith, Letter to Bishops on the Pastoral Care of Homosexual Persons (Oct. 1, 1985), 32 The Pope Speaks 62 (1987).

38. *Id.* A similar view can be found in Statement of Gordon B. Hinckley, Ensign, Nov. 1998, at 74, reproduced at http://www.mormon.org/question/faq/category/answer/0,9777,1601-1-60-1,00.html (accessed Nov. 21, 2002).

39. Paul Brest, The Supreme Court, 1975 Term—Foreword: In Defense of the Antidiscrimination Principle, 90 Harv. L. Rev. 1, 7–8 (1976).

40. Mark Twain, *The Adventures of Huckleberry Finn,* in *The Portable Mark Twain* 459 (Bernard DeVoto ed., 1946).

41. See William N. Eskridge Jr., No Promo Homo: The Sedimentation of Antigay Discourse and the Channeling Effect of Judicial Review, 75 N.Y.U. L. Rev. 1327, 1339–46 (2000).

42. M. J. Sydenham, *The French Revolution* 212 (1965).

43. See Steven D. Smith, Symbols, Perceptions, and Doctrinal Illusions: Establishment Neutrality and the 'No Endorsement' Test, 86 Mich. L. Rev. 266 (1987).

44. See *id.* at 325–31.

Chapter 5.
Against Blanket Nonrecognition

1. Paul Finkelman, *An Imperfect Union: Slavery, Federalism, and Comity* 296–310 (1981).

2. *Lemmon v. People,* 20 N.Y. 562, 602 (1860).

3. *Id.* at 603–6.

4. *Id.* at 630 (Wright, J., concurring), emphases in original.

5. *State v. Ross,* 76 N.C. 242, 250 (1877) (Reade, J., dissenting).

6. That is essentially what Virginia did say in the Miller-Jenkins case, described at the beginning of Chapter 8. Janet's parental relation to Isabella simply disappeared as soon as Isabella set foot in Virginia.

7. See Joseph W. Singer, Same Sex Marriage, Full Faith and Credit, and the Evasion of Obligation, 1 Stan. J. Civ. Rts. & Civ. Lib. 1, 13–18 (2005). I am here giving only the bare outlines of Lily and Anne's complex legal situation, which Singer lays out in detail. Of course, if the blanket rule of nonrecognition is rejected, then their legal situation becomes simpler and these inequities vanish.

8. Wash. Rev. Code §26.04.020. But see *Andersen v. King County,* 2004 WL 1738447 (Wash. Super. Ct., Aug. 4, 2004) (holding statute unconstitutional); *Castle v. State,* 2004 WL 1985215 (Wash. Super. Ct., Sept. 7, 2004) (same).

9. She might well have such obligations under the law of her home state even without a same-sex marriage. See *Elisa B. v. Superior Court,* 37 Cal. 4th 108, 33 Cal. Rptr. 3d 46, 117 P.3d 660 (2005) (imposing parental support obligation on a woman who agreed to raise children with her lesbian partner, supported her artificial insemination by an anonymous donor, and received the children into her home and held them out as her own). But a forum's public policy against same-sex marriage might still bar the recognition of parental rights arising out of a same-sex relationship.

10. This was the prospect presented to the English courts in the *Baindail* case, described at the beginning of Chapter 6.

11. See U.S. Const., Art. I, sec. 2, cl. 3 (counting slaves as three-fifths of a person for purposes of congressional representation); Art. I, sec. 9 (barring Congress from interfering with the slave trade until 1808); Art. IV, sec. 2, cl. 3 (guaranteeing return of fugitive slaves); Art. V (barring any amendment restricting the slave trade before 1808).

12. See Finkelman, *An Imperfect Union,* at 313–38.

13. Quoted in *id.* at 338 n.76.

14. *Bibb v. Navajo Freight Lines,* 359 U.S. 520 (1959).

15. *Crandall v. Nevada,* 73 U.S. (6 Wall.) 35 (1868). See also *Jones v. Helms,* 452 U.S. 412 (1981); *Shapiro v. Thompson,* 394 U.S. 618 (1969); *United States v. Guest,* 383 U.S. 745 (1966); *Edwards v. California,* 314 U.S. 160 (1941); *Dunn v. Blumstein,* 405 U.S. 330 (1972); *Memorial Hosp. v. Maricopa County,* 415 U.S. 250 (1974); *Saenz v. Roe,* 526 U.S. 489 (1999).

16. U.S. Const., amend. XIV, sec. 1.

17. 517 U.S. 620 (1996).

18. *Id.* at 624.

19. *Id.* at 632.

20. *Id.* at 630.

21. *Id.* at 635.

22. *Id.* at 634 (quoting *Department of Agriculture v. Moreno,* 413 U.S. 528, 534 [1973]).

23. This reading of *Romer* is elaborated and defended in Andrew Koppelman, *Romer v. Evans* and Invidious Intent, 6 Wm. & Mary Bill Rts. J. 89 (1997).

24. 539 U.S. 558 (2003).

25. *Id.* at 578.

26. *Id.* at 576.

27. *Id.* at 583 (O'Connor, J., concurring).

28. *Id.* (quoting *Romer,* 517 U.S. at 634).

29. *Lawrence,* 539 U.S. at 574.

30. See *Id.* at 570.

31. *Romer,* 517 U.S. at 633.

32. This interpretation of *Lawrence* is elaborated and defended in Andrew Koppelman, *Lawrence's* Penumbra, 88 Minn. L. Rev. 1171 (2004). For a state supreme court decision adopting a somewhat similar reading of *Lawrence,* see *Kansas v. Limon,* 122 P.3d 22 (Kan. 2005).

33. *Romer,* 517 U.S. at 636 (Scalia, J., dissenting).

34. *Id.* at 645.

35. *Id.* at 652.

36. See, e.g., Patrick Lee & Robert P. George, What Sex Can Be: Self-Alienation, Illusion, or One-Flesh Union, 42 Am. J. Juris. 135 (1997).

37. David A. Strauss, The Myth of Colorblindness, 1986 Sup. Ct. Rev. 99.

38. "[I]f the state needs no stronger justification for dealing with speech than it needs for dealing with other forms of conduct, then the principle of freedom of speech is only an illusion." Frederick Schauer, *Free Speech: A Philosophical Enquiry* 8 (1982). See also George Kateb, The Freedom of Worthless and Harmful Speech, in *Liberalism without Illusions* (Bernard Yack

ed., 1996); Andrew Koppelman, Does Obscenity Cause Moral Harm?, 105 Colum. L. Rev. 1635 (2005).

Chapter 6.
Choice of Law Rules

1. *Baindail v. Baindail,* [1946] P. 122, [1946] All E.R. 342, 344, CA.

2. See *Baindail v. Baindail,* [1945] 2 All E.R. 374.

3. L.R. 1 P. & D. 130, 14 L.T. 188 (1866).

4. *Id.* at 133.

5. *Id.* at 134.

6. 38 Ch. D. 220 (1887).

7. *Id.* at 236; emphasis in original.

8. J. H. C. Morris, The Recognition of Polygamous Marriages in English Law, 66 Harv. L. Rev. 961, 968 (1953).

9. Dennis Fitzpatrick, Non-Christian Marriage, 2 J. of Soc. of Comp. Leg. (2d ser.) 359, 379 (1900), quoted in *Id.* at 968.

10. This was noted in John Delatre Falconbridge, *Essays on the Conflict of Laws* 658 n. (1947).

11. See generally 2 Lawrence Collins, ed., *Dicey and Morris on the Conflict of Laws* 693–714 (13th ed. 2000).

12. As long ago as 1947, Falconbridge would say only that if the parties to a polygamous marriage "visited or took up their residence in England, whether they became domiciled there or not, they would probably be obliged to pay a decent measure of respect to English social customs, or, at least, not to conduct themselves in flagrant disregard of such customs." Falconbridge, *Essays,* at 659–60. Current treatises take for granted that polygamous marriages will exist and that the parties may cohabit in England: "Although the Rent Act and the Housing Acts are silent on the point, it is submitted that two widows who have been living together require the same protection against eviction from the former matrimonial home as one does and that the husband's tenancy should vest in them as joint tenants after his death." Nigel Lowe & Gillian Douglas, *Bromley's Family Law* 51 (9th ed. 1998).

13. Collins, ed., *Dicey and Morris,* at 707–14.

14. *Baindail,* [1946] All E.R. at 347.

15. A New York court was similarly inhospitable to a claim by a man who, after entering a potentially polygamous marriage in India, came to the United States and applied for a license to marry another woman. *Application of Sood,* 208 Misc. 819, 142 N.Y.S.2d 591 (Sup. Ct. 1955).

16. A black man who had married a white woman in Washington, one writer observed in 1905, could thereafter go to Virginia, where that marriage would be void, marry a black woman there, "and thereafter may divide his time between the two women, living in Virginia with the negress, his lawful Virginia wife, and in Washington with the white woman, his no less lawful Washington wife. Thus we may have legalized polygamy." Joseph R. Long, *A Treatise on the Law of Domestic Relations* 98 (1905). Neither state could prosecute the man for bigamy, for the second marriage would be no crime in Virginia, and Washington law would not apply to acts done in Virginia. "Of course, if either wife objected to the arrangement, she could get a divorce on the ground of adultery." *Id.*, n.29a. Story had similar worries about a blanket rule of nonrecognition:

> Suppose, for instance, a marriage celebrated in France according to the law of that country, should be held void in England, what would be the consequences? Each party might marry anew in the other country. In one country the issue would be deemed legitimate, in the other illegitimate. The French wife would in France be held the only wife, and entitled as such to all the rights of property appertaining to that relation. In England the English wife would hold the same exclusive rights and character. What then would be the confusion in regard to the personal property of the parties, in its own nature transitory, passing alternately from one country to the other! Suppose there should be issue of both marriages, and then all the parties should become domiciled in England or France, what confusion of rights, what embarrassments of personal and conjugal relations must necessarily be created! (Joseph Story, *Commentaries on the Conflict of Laws* 201 [8th ed. Melville Bigelow 1883])

17. *In re Dalip Singh Bir's Estate*, 188 P.2d 499 (Cal. App. 1948).

18. Restatement (Second) of Conflict of Laws, sec. 283(2) (1971).

19. See Symeon C. Symeonides, Choice of Law in the American Courts in 2003: Seventeenth Annual Survey, 52 Am. J. Comp. L. 9, 26 (2004); Symeon C. Symeonides, Choice of Law in the American Courts in 2000: As the Century Turns, 49 Am. J. Comp. L. 1, 13 (2001).

20. J. Philip Johnson, Note, The Validity of a Marriage under the Conflict of Laws, 38 N.D. L. Rev. 442, 454 (1962). However, marriage evasion statutes were adopted by other states, and fourteen still have them in some

form. See Homer H. Clark Jr., *The Law of Domestic Relations in the United States* 87 & n.52 (2d ed. 1988).

21. Restatement of Conflict of Laws, sec. 132 (1934).

22. "A marriage which satisfies the requirements of the state where the marriage was contracted will everywhere be recognized as valid unless it violates the strong public policy of another state which had the most significant relationship to the spouses and the marriage at the time of the marriage." Restatement (Second) of Conflict of Laws, sec. 283(2) (1971).

23. A comment attached to the provision noted that "differences among the marriage laws of various states usually involve only minor matters of debatable policy rather than fundamentals." *Id.*, comment h.

24. "All marriages contracted . . . outside this state, that were valid at the time of the contract or subsequently validated by the laws of the place in which they were contracted or by the domicile of the parties, are valid in this state." Uniform Marriage and Divorce Act, sec. 210, 9A U.L.A. 159, 194 (1998). (The act was promulgated in 1970.) The comment to this provision states that it "expressly fails to incorporate the 'strong public policy' exception of the Restatement and hence may change the law in some jurisdictions. This section will preclude invalidation of many marriages which would have been invalidated in the past." *Id.* The states that have adopted the act are Arizona, Colorado, Illinois, Kentucky, Minnesota, Missouri, Montana, and Washington (though Kentucky omits this provision). *Id.* Nearly half the states have this or similar language in their statutes. See Barbara J. Cox, Same-Sex Marriage and Choice-of-Law: If We Marry in Hawaii, Are We Still Married When We Return Home?, Wisc. L. Rev. 1033, 1066–68 (1994) (collecting statutes). Most of these states have, however, recently amended their laws to withhold recognition from same-sex marriages.

25. Douglas Laycock, Equal Citizens of Equal and Territorial States: The Constitutional Foundations of Choice of Law, 92 Colum. L. Rev. 249, 323 (1992).

26. The usefulness of the concept is questioned in Russell J. Weintraub, *Commentary on the Conflict of Laws* 13–51 (4th ed. 2001).

27. He acknowledges that "close cases will arise when citizens of different states see each other in both states and the relevant relationship cannot be confidently located in either." Laycock, Equal Citizens, at 325. Calvin Johnson has suggested in conversation that the court might look to the location of the couple's home, or (if they own more than one) of the more expensive home.

28. Eugene F. Scoles, Peter Hay, Patrick J. Borchers, & Symeon C. Symeonides, *Conflict of Laws* 562 (4th ed. 2004).

29. *Id.* at 561. The same approach is endorsed in George W. Stumberg, *Principles of Conflict of Laws* 288 (3d ed. 1963).

30. See J. E. Penner, The "Bundle of Rights" Picture of Property, 43 U.C.L.A. L. Rev. 711 (1996).

31. Scoles et al., *Conflict of Laws*, at 562.

32. Or there may not. Merrill and Smith note that the "bundle of rights" picture overlooks the value of having property come in standardized packages, since that makes it easy for third parties to learn what the rights of others are. Thomas W. Merrill & Henry E. Smith, What Happened to Property in Law and Economics?, 111 Yale L. J. 357 (2001). There is similar value in having relationships come in standardized packages.

33. *In re Estate of Lenherr,* 455 Pa. 225, 314 A.2d 255 (1974) (prohibited remarriage after divorce).

34. *Lenherr,* 314 A.2d at 258.

35. *Id.* at 259.

36. See Rep. No. 97-16 (Jan. 31, 1997), at http://www.gao.gov/archive/1997/og97016.pdf; updated by Rep. No. 04-353R (Jan. 4, 2004), at http://www.gao.gov/new.items/d04353r.pdf.

37. A short catalogue is in American Bar Association Section of Family Law, A White Paper: An Analysis of the Law Regarding Same-Sex Marriage, Civil Unions, and Domestic Partnerships, 38 Fam. L. Q. 339, 366–70 (2004). For more detailed analysis, see David L. Chambers, What If? The Legal Consequences of Marriage and the Legal Needs of Lesbian and Gay Male Couples, 95 Mich. L. Rev. 447 (1996).

38. Barbara J. Cox, Same-Sex Marriage and Choice-of-Law, 1033, 1063 n.168; see also *Id.* at 1092–93; Barbara Cox, Using an "Incidents of Marriage" Analysis When Considering Interstate Recognition of Same-Sex Couples' Marriages, Civil Unions, and Domestic Partnerships, 13 Widener L. J. 699 (2004).

39. Deborah M. Henson, Will Same-Sex Marriages Be Recognized in Sister States? Full Faith and Credit and Due Process Limitations on States' Choice of Law Regarding the Status and Incidents of Homosexual Marriages following Hawaii's Baehr v. Lewin, 32 U. Louisville J. Fam. L. 551, 564–66, 581–83 (1993–94).

40. "A court should compare the purposes of the invalidating rule with the marital incident in issue and not apply the invalidating rule if enjoyment of the incident would not substantially undermine those purposes. It is passing strange, for example, to deprive a woman, who has lived with a man as his wife for twenty years, of her 'widow's' claim to workers' compensation benefits on the ground that she was the decedent's first cousin or that

a ceremonial marriage was not performed." Weintraub, *Commentary on the Conflict of Laws*, at 294–95, footnote omitted.

41. Willis L. M. Reese, Marriage in American Conflict of Laws, 26 Int'l & Comp. L. Q. 952, 954 (1977).

Chapter 7.
When to (and When Not to)
Recognize Same-Sex Marriages

1. Kibret Markos, Killer Gets 30 Years, *The Record* (New Jersey), Apr. 16, 2004.

2. Quoted in Evan Wolfson, *Why Marriage Matters: America, Equality, and Gay People's Right to Marry* 127 (2004)

3. Dean Murphy, Death after Leg Surgery Surprises a Hit-and-Run Victim's Family, *N.Y. Times*, Feb. 17, 2002.

4. See *Prosser and Keeton on Torts*, § 127, at 947–49 (5th ed. 1984).

5. *Langan v. St. Vincent's*, 765 N.Y.S.2d 411, 422 (N.Y. Sup. Ct. 2003).

6. *Langan v. St. Vincent's*, 802 N.Y.S.2d 476 (N.Y. App. Div., 2d Dep't 2005).

7. See Chapter 9.

8. I borrow this useful nomenclature from Note, Developments in the Law—The Law of Marriage and Family: Constitutional Constraints on Interstate Same-Sex Marriage Recognition, 116 Harv. L. Rev. 2028, 2038 (2003).

9. Mass. Gen. Laws Ann. 207 § 11.

10. *Cote-Whitacre v. Dept. of Pub. Health*, 844 N.E. 2d 623 (Mass. 2006).

11. See Barbara J. Cox, Same-Sex Marriage and the Public Policy Exception in Choice-of-Law: Does It Really Exist?, 16 Quinnip. L. Rev. 61 (1996).

12. See *Lawrence v. Texas*, 539 U.S. 558 (2003).

13. Connecticut Att'y Gen. Op. (Aug. 2, 2004) (establishing that marriage licenses from Massachusetts of same-sex spouse would be recognized in Connecticut to change name on driver's license and car registrations); 2004 N.Y. Op. Att'y Gen. 1, 34–35 (Mar. 3, 2004) (R.A. 672–700) (stating that New York will recognize same-sex marriages legally performed elsewhere); Rhode Island Att'y Gen. Op. (Oct. 19, 2004) (stating that same-sex spouse married in Massachusetts would be eligible to receive spousal benefits under teacher's retirement system).

14. *Burns v. Burns*, 560 S.E.2d 47 (Ga. App. 2002).

15. *Wilson v. Ake*, 354 F.Supp.2d 1298 (M.D. Fla. 2005).

16. Similar reasoning controlled the *Lenherr* case, discussed in Chapter 6.

17. *Rosengarten v. Downes,* 802 A.2d 170 (Conn. App. 2002), cert. granted, 806 A.2d 1066 (2002); *Lane v. Albanese,* 2005 WL 896129 (Conn. Super. 2005).

18. *In re R.S. and J.A.,* No. F-185063 (Dist. Ct. Jefferson County, Tex., Mar. 3, 2003).

19. *In re KJB and JSP,* No. CDCD 119660 (Woodbury County Dist. Ct. Iowa, Nov. 14, 2003); Frank Santiago, Iowa Judge OK's Lesbian Divorce, *Des Moines Register,* Dec. 12, 2003, at 1A; *In re M. G. and S. G.,* No. 02-D-292 (Fam. Ct. W.Va., Jan. 3, 2003).

20. See Herma Hill Kay, Same-Sex Divorce in the Conflict of Laws, 15 King's College L. J. 63 (2004).

21. For similar analysis, see Barbara Cox, Using an "Incidents of Marriage" Analysis When Considering Interstate Recognition of Same-Sex Couples' Marriages, Civil Unions, and Domestic Partnerships, 13 Widener L. J. 699 (2004).

22. 539 U.S. 558 (2003).

23. See Eugene F. Scoles, Peter Hay, Patrick J. Borchers, & Symeon C. Symeonides, *Conflict of Laws* 974 (4th ed. 2004). On the Sunday restriction, see, e.g., *Cameron v. Gunstock Acres,* 348 N.E.2d 791 (Mass. 1976).

24. Thus, for example, if a Massachusetts couple moves to Illinois, and one spouse dies and leaves no inheritance to the other, the Illinois courts should give the survivor the amount of the elective share that a surviving spouse is entitled to under Illinois law. See 755 ILCS 5/2-8. Two unrelated people can enter into a contract whereby one promises to leave a bequest to the other, and if supported by consideration courts enforce such contracts by awarding "the value of the property which was to come to the promisee." Thomas E. Atkinson, *Handbook of the Law of Wills* §48, at 218 (2d ed. 1953). See, e.g., *Estate of Fritz,* 406 N.W.2d 475 (Mich. App. 1987). See generally Jesse Dukeminier et al., *Wills, Trusts, and Estates* 286–87 (7th ed. 2005).

25. This is advocated in F. A. Buckley & Larry Ribstein, Calling a Truce in the Marriage Wars, 2001 Ill. L. Rev. 561.

26. In some states this approach is apparently barred by statute. See Chapter 9.

27. There is now some authority to the contrary: the Connecticut attorney general and a tax court in New Jersey have both opined that, although those states recognize civil unions of gay people, they will give no effect whatsoever to Massachusetts or Canadian same-sex marriages. Connecticut Att'y Gen. Op., No. 2005-024 (Sept. 20, 2005); *Hennefeld v. Montclair,* 22 N.J. Tax 166,

178–84 (2005). But this is just blanket nonrecognition again. Attorney General Blumenthal was responding to a request from the Registrar of Vital Statistics, who wanted to know whether a couple who had entered into a foreign same-sex marriage or civil union could enter into a civil union in Connecticut with the same partner. Blumenthal's answer: no repeating civil unions, but a party to a foreign same-sex marriage "may obtain a Connecticut civil union because Connecticut courts will not recognize a same-sex marriage as either a civil union or a marriage." This logic can be deflated with a simple question: can someone who has entered into a foreign same-sex marriage enter into a civil union in Connecticut with a *different* partner? It is safe to presume that the Connecticut legislature did not intend to legalize polygamy.

28. *Pacific Gamble Robinson Co. v. Lapp*, 622 P.2d 850, 856 (Wash. 1980).

29. On the legal difficulties faced by same-sex couples with children in the federal system, see Deborah L. Forman, Interstate Recognition of Same-Sex Parents in the Wake of Gay Marriage, Civil Unions, and Domestic Partnerships, 46 B.C. L. Rev. 1 (2004).

30. A possible variant of this problem has been suggested by Prof. Ralph Whitten. Some states do not permit two single people to adopt the same child. If one of those states were to recognize same-sex marriage, then in that state marriage would be an essential predicate of an adoption by a same-sex couple. Other states with strong public policies against same-sex marriage might then refuse to recognize the marriage. Ralph G. Whitten, Full Faith and Credit for Dummies, 38 Creighton L. Rev. 465, 486 n.77 (2005). This problem is now entirely hypothetical, however, because no state that recognizes same-sex marriage has this kind of restriction on who may adopt.

31. See Seth Kreimer, Territoriality and Moral Dissensus: Thoughts on Abortion, Slavery, Gay Marriage and Family Values, 16 Quinnip. L. Rev. 161, 182–89 (1996).

32. The only case that has come close to addressing this problem recognized the parent-child relationship created by the foreign statute. *In re Doe*, 793 N.Y.S.2d 878 (N.Y. Sur. 2005). One state has, however, declared that it will not recognize adoptions by more than one person of the same sex from any other state, and the question is now being debated in the literature. Okla. Stat. Tit. 10, § 7502-1.4(A)(Supp. 2005); Robert G. Spector, The Unconstitutionality of Oklahoma's Statute Denying Recognition to Adoptions by Same-Sex Couples from Other States, 40 Tulsa L. Rev. 467 (2005); Lynn D. Wardle, A Critical Analysis of Interstate Recognition of Lesbigay Adoptions, 3 Ave Maria L. Rev. 561 (2005). As this book was going to press, the statute was held unconstitutional by a federal district court. *Finstuen v. Edmondson*, 2006 WL 1445354 (W.D. Okla. 2006).

33. 14 Fed. Cas. 602 (E.D. Va. 1879).

34. *Crandall v. Nevada*, 73 U.S. (6 Wall.) 35 (1868).

35. Thanks to Tobias Wolff for emphasizing this difficulty in conversation.

36. See Genesis 19:1–8, Judges 19:16–30. For an overview of contending interpretations, see Thomas Schmidt, *Straight and Narrow? Compassion and Clarity in the Homosexuality Debate* 30–32, 86–89 (1995).

Chapter 8.
The Irrelevance of Full Faith and Credit
and the Defense of Marriage Act

1. These quotations are drawn from Christina Nuckols, Two Women, Two States, One Child, *Virginian Pilot*, Dec. 13, 2004.

2. Jonathan Finer, Judge Claims Control of Same-Sex Custody Fight, *Wash. Post*, Sept. 9, 2004.

3. Adam Liptak, Custody after Civil Union Puts Two Rulings in Conflict, *N.Y. Times*, Sept. 8, 2005. It may be relevant that this was an evasive marriage, since the couple was originally domiciled in Virginia. A Vermont court might, however, reasonably decide that this impediment to the marriage was cured when the couple moved to Vermont. See Eugene F. Scoles, Peter Hay, Patrick J. Borchers, & Symeon C. Symeonides, *Conflict of Laws* 580-81 (4th ed. 2004).

4. 28 U.S.C. § 1738A.

5. This federal definition is entirely irrelevant here because DOMA does not purport to affect state law in any way with this provision.

6. 28 U.S.C. § 1738C.

7. The bill passed the House by a vote of 342–67 on July 12, 1996. 142 Cong. Rec. H7505–6. It passed the Senate by a vote of 85–14 on September 10, 1996. 142 Cong. Rec. S10129.

8. U.S. Const., Art. IV, sec. 1.

9. See act of May 26, 1790, ch. 11, 1 Stat. 122, codified at 28 U.S.C. § 1738; Willis M. Reese, Full Faith and Credit, in 3 *Encyclopedia of the American Constitution* 1170–71 (Leonard W. Levy & Kenneth W. Karst, eds., 2d ed. 2000); Lea Brilmayer, *Conflict of Laws* 298–307 (2d ed. 1995).

10. The misconceptions, and the futile attempts to clear up the mess, are amply documented in Patrick J. Borchers, The Essential Irrelevance of the Full Faith and Credit Clause to the Same-Sex Marriage Debate, 38 Creighton L. Rev. 353 (2005), and Ralph G. Whitten, Full Faith and Credit for Dummies, 38 Creighton L. Rev. 465 (2005).

11. A very few courts have embraced the proposition that full faith and credit requires courts to recognize out-of-state marriages that would not be permitted in the forum state. All of these cases involved common law marriages. And for some reason, all of them were decided by lower appellate courts in Louisiana. See *Wyble v. Minvielle*, 217 So.2d 684, 688 (La. App. 3d Cir. 1969); *Succession of Rodgers*, 499 So.2d 492, 495 (La. App. 2d Cir. 1986); *Netecke v. State*, 715 So.2d 449 (La. App. 3d Cir. 1998); *Fritsche v. Vermilion Parish Hospital Svc. Dist.*, 893 So.2d 935, 937–38 (La. App. 3d Cir. 2005). The first case in this sequence simply accepted the proposition with no authority except the text of the clause, and the later cases followed it with no additional analysis. Even if these cases are correctly decided, they are irrelevant to the same-sex marriage debate because they involve formal rather than substantive marriage conditions. Formal marriage conditions do not elicit strong public policy objections.

12. Emily J. Sack, Domestic Violence across State Lines: The Full Faith and Credit Clause, Congressional Power, and Interstate Enforcement of Protection Orders, 98 Nw. U. L. Rev. 827, 874–905 (2004).

13. *Sun Oil v. Wortman*, 486 U.S. 717, 729–30 n.3 (1988); see also *Id.* at 735 n.2 (Brennan, J., concurring in part and concurring in the judgment); *Allstate Insurance Co. v. Hague*, 449 U.S. 302, 308 n.10 (1981) (plurality opinion).

14. Both the Fifth Amendment, which restrains the federal government, and the Fourteenth Amendment, which restrains the states, provide that no person shall be deprived "of life, liberty, or property, without due process of law." U.S. Const., amends. 5, 14.

15. *International Shoe Co. v. State of Washington, Office of Unemployment Compensation and Placement*, 326 U.S. 310, 316 (1945) (quoting *Milliken v. Meyer*, 311 U.S. 457, 463 [1940]).

16. See *Grace v. MacArthur*, 170 F.Supp. 442 (E.D. Ark. 1959); see also *Burnham v. Superior Court*, 495 U.S. 604 (1990) (upholding constitutionality of jurisdiction over any party who is served with process while voluntarily present in forum state).

17. *Phillips Petroleum Co. v. Shutts*, 472 U.S. 797, 818 (1985) (quoting *Allstate*, 449 U.S. at 313).

18. See Ga. Code § 9-11-4(f) ("All process may be served anywhere within the territorial limits of the state").

19. Ga. Code § 19-3-3.1(b) provides: "No marriage between persons of the same sex shall be recognized as entitled to the benefits of marriage. Any marriage entered into by persons of the same sex pursuant to a marriage license issued by another state or foreign jurisdiction or otherwise shall be void in this state. Any contractual rights granted by virtue of such license shall be

unenforceable in the courts of this state and the courts of this state shall have no jurisdiction whatsoever under any circumstances to grant a divorce or separate maintenance with respect to such marriage or otherwise to consider or rule on any of the parties' respective rights arising as a result of or in connection with such marriage."

20. These hypotheticals are only for the sake of understanding the effects permitted by DOMA. I do not mean to insult the courts of Georgia by implying that they would cooperate with these disgusting stratagems. In other contexts, Georgia courts have not applied the public policy exception to ordinary choice of law principles when adjudicating transactions that occurred entirely outside of that state. See John Bernard Corr, Modern Choice of Law and Public Policy: The Emperor Has the Same Old Clothes, 39 U. Miami L. Rev. 647, 664–66 (1985) (collecting cases).

21. DOMA is a proviso to the full faith and credit statute, which provides generally that each state's "Acts, records and judicial proceedings . . . shall have the same full faith and credit in every court within the United States . . . as they have by law or usage in the courts of such State, Territory, or Possession from which they are taken." 28 U.S.C. § 1738(a). To the extent that DOMA is inapplicable, this statute remains in force.

22. It probably does not have such authority. See Andrew Koppelman, Dumb and DOMA: Why the Defense of Marriage Act Is Unconstitutional, 83 Iowa L. Rev. 1, 18–24 (1997).

23. *Fauntleroy v. Lum,* 210 U.S. 230 (1908).

24. See Brilmayer, *Conflict of Laws,* at 298–99.

25. Habib A. Balian, Note, 'Til Death Do Us Part: Granting Full Faith and Credit to Marital Status, 68 S. Cal. L. Rev. 397 (1995); Deborah M. Henson, Will Same-Sex Marriages Be Recognized in Sister States? Full Faith and Credit and Due Process Limitations on States' Choice of Law Regarding the Status and Incidents of Homosexual Marriages following Hawaii's Baehr v. Lewin, 32 U. Louisville J. Fam. L. 551, 588 (1993–94). This stratagem has been proposed before, as a way of thwarting the southern states' nonrecognition of interracial marriages, but it does not appear ever to have been tried. See Albert A. Ehrenzweig, Miscegenation in the Conflict of Laws: Law and Reason Versus the Restatement Second, 45 Cornell L. Q. 659, 662 (1960).

26. House Judiciary Committee, 104th Cong., 2d Sess., Report to Accompany Defense of Marriage Act, H.R. Rep. 104-664 (July 9, 1996), at 30; reprinted in 1996 U.S.C.C.A.N. 2905.

27. *Id.* The report goes on to note, however, that the act's effect "is merely to authorize a sister State to decline to give effect to such orders; it does not mandate that outcome, and, indeed, given the special status of ju-

dicial proceedings, the Committee expects that States will honor judicial orders as long as it can do so without surrendering its public policy against same-sex marriages." *Id.* States would, of course, have unfettered discretion to determine how sweeping their public policies were in such cases.

28. "Generally speaking, a judgment is of no legal concern to a person who is neither a party to it nor otherwise bound by it under the rules of res judicata. A judgment determines issues and claims only among those who are so bound and does not preclude another person from litigating the same issues afresh, nor does it preclude him from enforcing claims that are inconsistent with those that have been adjudicated. So far as such a third person is concerned, a judgment between others has no greater effect than a contract or conveyance between others. Ordinarily, therefore, he can simply ignore it in connection with the assertion of his own rights." Restatement (Second) of Judgments (1982), sec. 76, comment a. Even if a person would ordinarily be bound by a judgment, "[i]t is clear that the represented person should be able to set aside a judgment that was procured by collusion between the person representing him and the opposing party. No worthy interest is served by sustaining such a judgment, and both private and public interests would be violated if the judgment were given effect in the face of such an attack." *Id.,* sec. 75, comment c. David Currie has observed that foreign judgments are entitled to conclusive effect precisely because their adversarial nature guarantees that the party who stands to benefit under the appropriate law has the necessary incentive to insist on its application. These considerations do not apply to garden variety administrative actions, such as marriages; they similarly do not apply to collusive judgments. David P. Currie, Full Faith and Credit to Marriages, 1 Green Bag 2d 7 (1997).

Mark Rosen, in the most sophisticated defense of DOMA that has yet been written, has argued that the judgments provision of the statute should be read *only* to reach such collusive judgments, because they were the ones upon which Congress's attention was focused. Mark D. Rosen, Why the Defense of Marriage Act is Not (Yet?) Unconstitutional: *Lawrence,* Full Faith and Credit, and the Many Societal Actors that Determine What the Constitution Requires, 90 Minn. L. Rev. 915 (2006). He advocates "interpreting DOMA more narrowly than its plain language admittedly suggests," *id.* at 981, and avoiding the plain language's unreasonable and unjust results "because Congress did not contemplate such an application during the course of DOMA's debate and enactment." *Id.* at 980. This implicitly relies on a novel and strange principle of statutory interpretation: an unambiguous statute will not be construed to reach a situation if that situation was not specifically considered during the legislative history. It would follow that a broad statute passed with little reflection or debate has no applications at all.

29. 517 U.S. 620 (1996).

30. 539 U.S. 558 (2003).

31. See, e.g., Ralph U. Whitten, Exporting and Importing Domestic Partnerships: Some Conflict-of-Laws Questions and Concerns, 2001 B.Y.U. L. Rev. 1235.

32. Some evidence in the legislative history supports this interpretation. After struggling in vain to compile evidence of any real danger that full faith and credit might obligate the entire country to recognize same-sex marriage for all purposes, the House Judiciary Committee report on the bill concludes with the argument that the "[m]ost important" reason for legislative action is "the evident disquiet in the various States created by the Hawaii situation." Noting that many states had recently passed statutes declaring that they would not recognize same-sex marriages valid in other states, the report concludes: "The fact that these States are sufficiently concerned about their ability to defend their marriage laws against the threat posed by the Hawaii situation is enough to persuade the Committee that federal legislation is warranted. The States, after all, are best-positioned to assess the legal situation within their own State; that so many of them are not content to rely on the amorphous 'public policy' exception reveals that congressional clarification and assistance is both necessary and appropriate." House Judiciary Committee, Report, at 9–10. A more carefully drafted statute might have provided the intended clarification.

33. See, e.g., *United States v. Seeger,* 380 U.S. 163 (1965); *Welsh v. United States,* 398 U.S. 333 (1970).

34. See, e.g., *Morton v. Mancari,* 417 U.S. 535, 549–50 (1974).

35. Norman J. Singer, 2 *Sutherland's Statutes and Statutory Construction* § 46.07 (6th ed. 2000).

36. 1 William Blackstone, *Commentaries on the Laws of England* 91 (8th ed. 1778).

37. Singer, *Sutherland's Statutes and Statutory Construction* § 46.06.

38. Statement by President George W. Bush, Feb. 24, 2004.

39. Pub. L. 104-199; 110 Stat. 2419; 1 U.S.C. 7.

40. See 11 U.S.C. § 523(a)(5).

41. See 5 U.S.C. § 8901.

42. See 5 U.S.C. § 8701.

43. See 5 U.S.C. § 8101–8151.

44. See 17 U.S.C. § 304.

45. See 12 U.S.C. § 1701j-3(d).

46. See 29 U.S.C. § 2612(a)(1)(C).

47. See 42 U.S.C. § 402 et seq.

48. The General Accounting Office has compiled a much more extensive list of affected federal benefits. See U.S. General Accounting Office, Defense of Marriage Act (Jan. 31, 1997).

49. The Court has held that the due process clause of the Fifth Amendment constrains Congress in the same way that the equal protection clause of the Fourteenth Amendment constrains the states. See *Adarand Constructors, Inc. v. Pena,* 515 U.S. 200, 214–19 (1995); *Bolling v. Sharpe,* 347 U.S. 497, 500 (1954).

50. See *Loving v. Virginia,* 388 U.S. 1 (1967).

51. *Romer,* 517 U.S. at 633.

52. The closest thing to such a justification that was offered was that many such policies give married couples claims on the federal fisc, and that recognizing same-sex marriages would cost the government money. Senator Phil Gramm warned that the "failure to pass this bill . . . will create . . . a whole group of new beneficiaries—no one knows what the number would be— tens of thousands, hundreds of thousands, potentially more—who will be beneficiaries of newly created survivor benefits under Social Security, Federal retirement plans, and military retirement plans." Cong. Rec., daily ed. Sept. 10, 1996, at S10106. Such claims sometimes took a hysterical tone: Senator Robert Byrd said that he did "not think . . . that it is inconceivable that the costs associated with such a change could amount to hundreds of millions of dollars, if not billions—if not billions—of Federal taxpayer dollars." *Id.* at S10111.

53. *Romer,* 517 U.S. at 633.

54. *Id.* at 635.

55. House Judiciary Committee, Report, at 29.

56. House Judiciary Committee, Report, at 29; Prepared Statement of Professor Lynn D. Wardle (hereinafter Wardle statement), in Committee on the Judiciary, U.S. Senate, 104th Cong., 2d Sess., Hearing on Defense of Marriage Act, July 11, 1996 (S.Hrg. 104-533, Serial No. J-104-90) (hereinafter Senate Hearing), at 27.

57. Wardle statement at 27 n.4.

58. Prepared statement of Senator Don Nickles, one of the original sponsors of DOMA, in Senate Hearing, at 18.

59. *Romer,* 517 U.S. at 635.

60. See Daniel R. Ortiz, The Myth of Intent in Equal Protection, 41 Stan. L. Rev. 1105 (1989).

61. *Romer,* 517 U.S. at 633.

62. *Id.,* quoting *Louisville Gas & Elec. Co. v. Coleman,* 277 U.S. 32, 37–38 (1928).

63. The House Judiciary Committee report included a section on *Romer,* but it was primarily devoted to denouncing the opinion rather than extracting a principle from it and showing that principle's inapplicability to DOMA. See House Judiciary Committee, Report, at 30–32.

64. *Romer,* 517 U.S. at 633.

65. Statement of Senator Orrin Hatch, Chairman, Committee on the Judiciary, in Senate Hearing, at 2.

66. *Romer,* 517 U.S. at 633.

67. *Id.* at 635.

68. *Id.*

69. *Id.* at 632.

70. Michael C. Dorf, Facial Challenges to State and Federal Statutes, 46 Stan. L. Rev. 235, 279 (1994).

71. The only time this question was squarely presented to U.S. policy-makers, unencumbered by the distraction of interstate recognition, was after the terrorist attacks of September 11, 2001, when decisions had to be made about which bereaved families should receive compensation. In the end, awards were given to partners in same-sex relationships. See Jane Gross, U.S. Fund for Tower Victims Will Aid Some Gay Partners, *N.Y. Times,* May 30, 2002, at A1.

72. *Romer,* 517 U.S. at 635.

73. Dorf, Facial Challenges, at 279 n.192.

74. "In determining whether the invalid portion of a statute may be severed from the valid portion, the question is whether the legislature, if partial invalidity had been foreseen, would have wished the statute to be enforced with the invalid part excised or rejected altogether." Singer, *Sutherland's Statutes and Statutory Construction,* § 44:4, at 559–60. A law is not severable if "by sustaining only a part of the statute, the purpose of the act is changed or altered." *Id.,* § 44:7, at 583. But absent gay exclusion, the Romeo and Juliet provision is "independent of the invalid portion and . . . form[s] a complete act within itself"; *Id.,* § 44:4, at 562–66, so severance would hardly "defeat the intent of the legislature." *Id.,* § 44:8, at 588. "There is . . . a presumption that a legislative body generally intends its enactments to be severable, especially in the case where it will preserve the constitutionality of the enactment." *Id.,* § 44:3, at 556–57.

75. The argument of this paragraph is developed at greater length in Koppelman, Dumb and DOMA, at 28–32.

76. Roper Ctr. for Pub. Opinion Res., Question ID No. USP-SRNEW.020704, R14E, Feb. 2004, Westlaw, POLL Database. See also Chapter 4, note 12.

Chapter 9.
The Difference the Mini-DOMAs Make

1. The texts of almost all these provisions are compiled in Andrew Koppelman, Interstate Recognition of Same-Sex Marriages and Civil Unions: A Handbook for Judges, 153 U. Pa. L. Rev. 2143, 2165–94 (2005). Since that article was published, Texas has supplemented its statute with a constitutional amendment, discussed infra text accompanying note 32.

2. See, e.g., N.H. Rev. Stat. Ann. 457:1 (2001) ("No man shall marry . . . any other man"); 457:2 (2001) ("No woman shall marry . . . any other woman").

3. See, e.g., Ariz. Rev. Stat. sec. 25-101 (C) (West 2000) ("Marriage between persons of the same sex is void and prohibited"); Del. Code Ann. sec. 13-101(a) (1999) ("A marriage is prohibited and void . . . between persons of the same gender"); 750 Ill. Comp. Stat. 5/212 (West 1999) ("The following marriages are prohibited . . . a marriage between 2 individuals of the same sex").

4. What the reporter for the Restatement (Second) of Conflict of Laws wrote in another context is relevant here: "The fact that the statute contains no [choice of law] provision is persuasive evidence that the Legislature never gave thought to the question whether the statute should, or should not, be applied to foreign facts. At the least, there is no legislative command on the point and the court therefore enjoys some freedom of choice. It should be free, and indeed obliged, to inquire whether the value of applying the local statute and thus implementing the statutory policy is not outweighed by other choice-of-law considerations." Willis L. M. Reese, Marriage in American Conflict of Laws, 26 Int'l & Comp. L. Q. 952, 960 (1977).

5. See, e.g., Alaska Stat. 25.05.013 (Michie 2004) ("A marriage entered into by persons of the same sex, either under common law or under statute, that is recognized by another state or foreign jurisdiction is void in this state"); Ariz. Rev. Stat. sec. 25-112 (West 2000) ("Marriages valid by the laws of the place where contracted are valid in this state, except marriages that are void and prohibited by [statute against same-sex marriage]").

6. See, e.g., Idaho Code 32-209 (Michie 1996) ("All marriages contracted without this state, which would be valid by the laws of the state or country in which the same were contracted, are valid in this state, unless they violate the public policy of this state. Marriages that violate the public policy

of this state include, but are not limited to, same-sex marriages, and marriages entered into under the laws of another state or country with the intent to evade the prohibitions of the marriage laws of this state"); 750 Ill. Comp. Stat. 5/213.1 (West 1999) ("A marriage between 2 individuals of the same sex is contrary to the public policy of this State").

7. See William N. Eskridge Jr., Philip P. Frickey, & Elizabeth Garrett, *Legislation and Statutory Interpretation* 283–85 (2000).

8. See 1 Chester G. Vernier, *American Family Laws* 204–09 (1931) (compiling statutes). For earlier surveys to the same effect, see Note, Intermarriage with Negroes—A Survey of State Statutes, 36 Yale L. J. 858 (1927); 1 F. J. Stimson, *American Statute Law* 667–69 (1886).

9. See *Caballero v. Executor,* 24 La. Ann. 573 (1872) (La. Civ. Code sec. 95 [1838] declared interracial marriages "forbidden," "void," and a "nullity"); *Whittington v. McCaskill,* 65 Fla. 162, 163–64, 61 So. 236 (1913) (state constitution declared interracial marriages "forever prohibited" and statute deemed them "utterly null and void"); *Miller v. Lucks,* 203 Miss. 824, 831, 36 So. 2d 140, 3 A.L.R.2d 236 (1948) (state constitution declared such marriages "unlawful and void"). The leading cases in which the courts split on migratory marriages involved statutes with virtually identical language. *State v. Ross,* 76 N.C. 242 (1877), which recognized a migratory marriage, involved a statute that declared that "[a]ll marriages . . . between a white person and a free negro . . . shall be void" N.C. Rev. Code 68:7 (Little, Brown 1855). The law in *State v. Bell,* 66 Tenn. (7 Baxter) 9 (1872), which withheld recognition, was not materially different: "the intermarriage of white persons with negroes . . . is hereby prohibited." Tenn. Acts. 1869–70 at 69 (1870).

10. See *State v. Fenn,* 92 P. 417, 419 (Wash. 1907): "If the statute should be construed to avoid marriages contracted in other states by citizens of other states who never owed allegiance to our laws, it is the most drastic piece of legislation to be found on the statute books of any of our states. . . . [A] statute declaring marriages void, regardless of where contracted and regardless of the domicile of the parties, would be an anomaly and so far reaching in its consequences that a court would feel constrained to limit its operation, if any other construction were permissible."

11. Me. Rev. Stat. Ann. tit. 19-A, § 701 (West 1998).

12. See, e.g., Ky. Const. § 233A ("A legal status identical or substantially similar to that of marriage for unmarried individuals shall not be valid or recognized"); Neb. Const. Art. I, § 29 ("The uniting of two persons of the same sex in a civil union, domestic partnership, or other similar same-sex relationship shall not be valid or recognized in Nebraska").

13. Alas. Stat. § 25.05.013.

14. See Minn. Stat. Ann. § 517.03 (West. Supp. 2005) ("A marriage entered into by persons of the same sex, either under common law or statute, that is recognized by another state or foreign jurisdiction is void in this state and contractual rights granted by virtue of the marriage or its termination are unenforceable in this state"); Va. Code. Ann. § 20-45.2 (Michie 2004) ("A marriage between persons of the same sex is prohibited. Any marriage entered into by persons of the same sex in another state or jurisdiction shall be void in all respects in Virginia and any contractual rights created by such marriage shall be void and unenforceable").

15. Arkansas has a modified version of the language that is a bit clearer, referring to "contractual or other rights" granted by virtue of the marriage license, but it remains obscure what the reference to contract is intended to accomplish. Ark. Code Ann. § 9-11-208(c) (Michie 2002) ("Any marriage entered into by persons of the same sex, where a marriage license is issued by another state or by a foreign jurisdiction, shall be void in Arkansas and any contractual or other rights granted by virtue of that license, including its termination, shall be unenforceable in the Arkansas courts"). Contrast *id.,* § 9-11-208(d) ("nothing in this section shall prevent an employer from extending benefits to persons who are domestic partners of employees").

16. See Linda Silberman, Same-Sex Marriage: Refining the Conflict of Laws Analysis, 153 U. Pa. L. Rev. 2195, 2212 (2005).

17. Contrast Ohio, which specifically provides that its mini-DOMA should not be construed to "[a]ffect the validity of private agreements that are otherwise valid under the laws of this state." Ohio. Rev. Code Ann. § 3101.01(C)(3)(b) (West 2005).

18. Va. Code. Ann. § 20-45.3 (Michie 2004).

19. Laura Hutchison, Couple Feels Forced to Leave, *Fredericksburg Free Lance-Star,* Jan. 9, 2005.

20. Mont. Code Ann. § 40-1-401 (2003).

21. Mich. Const., Art. I, § 25.

22. 517 U.S. 620 (1996).

23. *Id.* at 632.

24. *Id.* at 630.

25. *Id.* at 635.

26. *Id.*

27. Fla. Stat. Ann. § 741.212(2) (West Supp. 2005); Ga. Const., Art. 1, § 4, para. 1(b); Ohio. Rev. Code Ann. § 3101.01(C)(4) (West 2005); Tex. Fam. Code Ann. § 6/204(c)(1) (Vernon Supp. 2004–05); W. Va. Code Ann. § 48-2-603 (Michie 2004).

28. Fla. Stat. Ann. § 741.212(1) (West Supp. 2005) ("Marriages between

persons of the same sex entered into in any jurisdiction, whether within, or outside the State of Florida, the United States, or any other jurisdiction, either domestic or foreign … are not recognized for any purpose in this state"); Ky. Rev. Stat. Ann. § 402.045(2) (Michie 1999) ("Any rights granted by virtue of [a same-sex] marriage, or its termination, shall be unenforceable in Kentucky courts"); La. Const., Art. XII, § 15 ("No official or court of the state of Louisiana shall recognize any marriage contracted in any other jurisdiction which is not the union of one man and one woman"); Ohio Rev. Code Ann. § 3101.01(C)(2) (West 2005) ("Any marriage entered into by persons of the same sex in any other jurisdiction shall be considered and treated in all respects as having no legal force or effect in this state and shall not be recognized by this state"). The Louisiana statute is quoted and discussed below.

29. La. Civ. Code Art. 3519.

30. La. Civ. Code Art. 3520.

31. As noted in the text, article 3520(A) provides that public policy can invalidate a marriage, but only if it is the public policy of the most interested state under article 3519. However, article 3520(B) evidently modifies this rule, declaring: "A purported marriage between persons of the same sex violates a strong public policy of the state of Louisiana and such a marriage contracted in another state and shall not be recognized in this state for any purpose, including the assertion of any right or claim as a result of the purported marriage."

32. Tex. Const., art. I, sec. 32. The bill proposing the amendment also contained the following language, which suggested that the drafters did have some sober moments: "This state recognizes that through the designation of guardians, the appointment of agents, and the use of private contracts, persons may adequately and properly appoint guardians and arrange rights relating to hospital visitation, property, and the entitlement to proceeds of life insurance policies without the existence of any legal status identical or similar to marriage." Tx. H.J.R. 6 (2005); Tx. Acts 2003, 78th Leg., ch. 124.

Chapter 10.
Toward Benign Competition

1. E. J. Graff, *What Is Marriage For?* 43 (1999). Horror stories of this kind are unfortunately not just hypothetical. See George Chauncey, *Why Marriage? The History Shaping Today's Debate over Gay Equality* 114–16 (2004).

2. See Paul H. Robinson, *Criminal Law Defenses* §131(c)–(d) (1984).

3. I know this sounds like something I made up, but see *People v. Seiber*, 394 N.E. 2d 1044 (Ill. App. Ct. 1979); *People v. Glenn*, 417 N.Y.S.2d 934 (N.Y. App. Div. 1979), rev'd on other grounds, 418 N.E.2d 1316; *State v. Collins*, 306 So.2d 662 (La. 1975).

4. See Lynn Waddell, Gays in Florida Seek Adoption Alternatives, *N.Y. Times*, Jan. 21, 2005.

5. See Paul Finkelman, *An Imperfect Union: Slavery, Federalism, and Comity* 297 (1981).

6. 844 N.E. 2d 623 (2006).

7. *Id.* at 645 (Spina, J., concurring).

8. *Id.* Full disclosure: I signed a brief in the case (see the next note), and an argument of mine was relied on by the dissenting opinion. Justice Ireland's dissent argued that if it was sex discrimination for Massachusetts to deny same-sex couples the right to marry, it was also sex discrimination to deny out-of-state same-sex couples the right to marry. See id. at 662–63 (Ireland, J., dissenting) (citing Andrew Koppelman, Same-Sex Marriage and Public Policy: The Miscegenation Precedents, 16 Quinnip. L. Rev. 105, 109 n.13 (1996)). This is correct, but the earlier *Goodridge* case was not decided on the basis of a sex discrimination argument, and in fact it had specifically rejected that argument. See *Goodridge v. Dept. of Public Health*, 798 N.E. 2d 941, 992 n. 13 (Mass. 2003). Justice Greaney, who had advanced that argument in *Goodridge*, concurred in the result in *Cote-Whitacre*.

9. An amicus brief that I joined emphasized this. See Brief of Amici Curiae of Professors of Conflict of Laws and Family Law, *Cote-Whitacre v. Dept. of Pub. Health* (signed by 24 law professors). None of the concurring opinions confronted this difficulty.

10. A 2003 Gallup poll found that only 39 percent of all respondents thought that same-sex marriage should be legally valid, but it also found that same-sex marriage was supported by 61 percent of eighteen- to twenty-nine-year-olds. See Linda Lyons, U.S. Next Down the Aisle toward Gay Marriage?, www.gallup.com (accessed Nov. 11, 2003). Recent polls suggest that opposition to same-sex marriage is declining rapidly. The Pew Research Center found that opposition to same-sex marriage dropped from 63% in February 2004 to 51% in March 2006, while support for such marriages rose from 29% in August 2004 to 39% in March 2006. Those who "strongly oppose" same-sex marriage dropped from 42% in February 2004 to 28% in March 2006. The decline was sharpest among senior citizens, Republicans, and Catholics and non-evangelical Protestants. Pew Research Center Survey Report, Less Opposition to Gay Marriage, Adoption, and Military Service, March 22, 2006.

Index